Healing Doesn't Look *Like That*

A SELF-DISCOVERY JOURNEY
TO JOY AND INNER PEACE WHILE HEALING FROM CODEPENDENCY.

Healing Doesn't Look Like That

TANESHIA **JOHNSON**, MSW

TJ SELFCARE PUBLISHING

Concord, California

HEALING DOESN'T LOOK LIKE THAT:
A self-discovery journey to joy and inner peace while healing from codependency

To request permissions, please contact the publisher at:
TJ SELFCARE PUBLISHING
taneshia@tjselfcare.com

Paperback ISBN: 979-8-21837695-6
First Paperback Edition: May 2024.

Edited by: Lyric Dodson, the Artful Editor & Monique D. Mensah
Cover by: Make Your Mark Publishing Solutions
Layout by: Make Your Mark Publishing Solutions

Contents

PART 3

Reconnect with Yourself and Your Needs

PART 4

Repair and Unlearn

Acknowledgements

want to acknowledge God for helping me write this book. I was scared to tell this story. Every time I prayed; God reassured me this story would one day help others heal. Thank you to my therapist, whom I wish I could name in this book. Your guidance and ability to listen and help me process my feelings and thoughts was truly a Godsend. I am thankful for the healing and growth I have accomplished in my life thanks to your help and healing energy. I acknowledge my developmental editor, Lyric Dodson, and my self-publishing assistant and copy editor, Monique D. Mensah, for their guidance, patience, and support. I thank and acknowledge both my parents. I thank my dad for allowing me to tell this story. In my heart, I believe he always knew our story would be a father-daughter love story that would one day help the world.

Dedication

To my readers, I pray my transparency blesses you and gives you the courage to make the necessary changes in your life to live as your true authentic self.

To all my friends and family, I love you. Thank you for loving me through hard times. I know you may not have realized I was going through some of the things you read in this book. Know that your love, patience, and loving energy was the only reason I was able to share this story with the rest of the world.

Note from the Author

want to start by being honest with you. I was afraid to write this book. As always, when I write, my intent is to bring the knowledge I have about codependency and people pleasing to you in a way that supports your healing journey. I want you to feel like you are reading the words of someone who has taken the time to do the research for you and is now giving you the gems you need to apply toward your own life.

When I originally wrote this book, it was too long and had too much dialogue. It felt more like a grad school paper than a book. After three edits, three years, and countless nights of tears, I decided that I am a storyteller. I couldn't share with you how complex it felt to heal from codependency without giving you the story behind my own healing journey.

When I first started my journey of healing, I was attending codependent anonymous meetings. I watched people of all walks of life come in and out of those meetings. Many of them had smiles so big that I envied them. I would ask them how they could smile through such pain, and they said one day I would find my own rhythm in life. I would understand my needs and no longer feel stuck in my thoughts and feelings. I waited five years to experience that feeling, but it never came. Every week felt like a routine I had grown tired of—get up, go to work, read my Bible, pray, go to therapy, go to a support meeting, and repeat. But one day, everything clicked. I pray this book gives you that "click," with epiphanies along the way.

I have added a QR code in the back of this book for you to download a worksheet to help you reflect on your own healing. My goal for you is that every page you read will bring you closer to your own healing journey, and when things feel hard, you can rest in knowing I have experienced the pain of growing and healing with you, and you will be okay.

PART
1

Dealing with Feelings of Rejection and Abandonment

Smile, It Confuses People

started off the year going to see my dad. My therapist and I had been talking a lot about me processing my feelings about my childhood with my parents instead of internalizing them. After reading hundreds of self-help books and going to therapy and codependency support groups for five years, I had determined that true recovery from codependency would involve me healing from past feelings of rejection and abandonment. To do this, I had to share with my parents that I never felt important or valued growing up. I had been dreading doing this work for a while, but I found there were only so many affirmations and so much journaling I could do. To heal, I had to do the work. And in this case, that meant confronting both of them and being open to their feelings while I shared mine.

My mother was the easy parent. Her two jobs took all her time when I was a child, and we didn't spend as much time together as we would've liked. With her, it was about finding more ways to bond and connect.

With my dad, though, it was much different. My feelings of abandonment and rejection were stronger. In my mind, my father's truth was that he really didn't want me and felt an obligation to take care of me. That he had no real desire to be my father. Reflecting on those thoughts for too long often brought me to tears, and it just felt easier not knowing the truth. But I was finding that this situation was bigger than my parents or the disappointment I might feel from their responses. It was about me getting the information I needed to heal my inner child and move on with my life. This wasn't a conversation I or my therapist thought I should have over the phone, so I took it upon myself to purchase a ticket to Florida to see my dad face to face.

Now, I've heard stories of me seeing my dad at two and three years old, but the first memory I have is from when I was six. My mother had been telling me I was going to see my dad for about two months. In my six-year-old mind, I didn't know why I had to go anywhere to see him. How come he wasn't coming to me, and I stay the night at his house or, better yet, how come he didn't live with me, my mom, and great aunt? Asking too many questions in my house could lead to a spanking. My family believed a child should not know too much about adult issues, so getting an explanation at six years old about why my dad wasn't with us wasn't realistic.

I just stood somewhere, lurking in the corners of our apartment like a mouse, watching my mother pack my luggage. I remember feeling confused and scared about where I was going and looking down in my suitcase, seeing new clothes, shorts, cute summer dresses, short-sleeved tops, and sandals. My entire life, I had lived in San Francisco, California, where summertime meant a high of seventy degrees in the day and forty to fifty degrees at night. I normally wore sweaters and jeans all year round. I didn't want to see my dad and didn't understand why I would need new clothes. Every time my mother brought it up to me, I wanted to say I didn't want to go, but I got the sense that I didn't have that option.

Days passed, and my mother and I were headed to the airport. As we walked to the gate, we met with a brown-skinned woman with an afro, wearing a blue skirt and a blazer with a Delta pin on the lapel. My mom and the woman exchanged words and smiles, and then next thing I knew, my mom was looking at me with a firm face, telling me to be good and that she loved me. The flight attendant took my hand, and we walked back to the plane.

Even though this was my first time on a plane, I didn't cry. My excitement was too great. I felt special because everyone else was waiting in line, but I got first dibs at a window seat and the snacks! It had been my experience with other adults that if they didn't want to take care of me, they would look mean and angry. It would make me scared, and I would often find ways to take care of myself or stay out of their way. But it wasn't like that with the flight attendant. She looked down at me often and always had a smile. She even asked me how I felt, and I got to choose my snacks and what movie I wanted to watch. I felt safe with her, and amid being scared about meeting my dad for the first time, safe was a good feeling.

The other flight attendants were nice too. Everyone grinned and checked on me. As we took off, one of them gave me head-phones to listen to a movie and extra snacks. I even sat in the back with them. It really made me feel special. I smiled every time the first flight attendant came by to check on me, and she smiled back. I feared being on the plane by myself, but she made the flight much easier. When we landed, the plane moved left to right a lot, and I got scared, but she held my hand and told me it would be okay.

As we deboarded the plane, the same flight attendant held my hand and brought me outside to meet my dad. I remember not wanting to let go of her hand, even though I didn't know her ... I didn't know my dad either. At least she seemed nice. I had no idea who my dad was.

As she and I glanced over the crowd, I saw a man who looked a lot like me. He stood 6'3" with dark skin, a mustache, and glasses, and he was wearing jeans and a t-shirt. He waved at me and her. She looked down at me, asking me if that was my dad. I looked at the man, confused about whether it was him or not. He had a big smile and started walking closer, so I assumed it was him.

"Taneshia Johnson," I heard a deep voice say.

My dad took my hand from the flight attendant. They greeted each other, and he took my sweater from her hand. We began walking away from the gate. I looked back, wishing I could return with her and go home, but I knew that wasn't an option.

"Welcome to Huntsville, Alabama, daughter! This summer is gonna be great!" he said.

I looked up at him, amazed at how much he looked like me. We even had the same nose. I stared at his fingers and saw that they looked like mine too. My face felt flat and emotionless; I wanted to cry because I wanted to go home. I didn't know him, and it terrified me to think about staying with him all summer.

I was taught crying would get me nowhere, so it was best to just put on a smile and be strong.

To my surprise, he saw my face and stopped walking. He pulled me to the side, got down on his knees and said, "Aw, come on, baby, give your daddy a big smile. It's going to be all right. You're gonna have fun."

I didn't believe him, but I was afraid to express my real feelings, so I smiled up at him and said, "Okay."

That experience with my dad became the regular way I interacted with him from age six years old until now. I never shared my real feelings. I took the love he gave and never asked for more. Parts of me felt lucky to have a dad. So many of my friends grew up with only one parent. But even as a child, I knew something was off. I mean he helped create me; I was part of him. I didn't understand how he was okay with not being a part of my life on a regular basis. Shouldn't he have wanted to nurture and take care of something that was a part of him? I had been trying to conceptualize this for decades. I concluded that figuring everything out on my own was not fair to me. It was time to ask my father where he'd been and tell him what I needed.

Through self-help books, therapy, and prayer, I was starting to see that I had never emotionally developed into a woman. The negative self-talk, feelings of inadequacy, and longing to be loved all stemmed from that six-year-old version of myself that never got a chance to be a kid.

My childhood was very structured. I would even say I was more like a "little adult" than a kid. With my father living in Alabama and my mother and I living in California, my mother was left to play the role of a single parent. She received support from my great aunt to help raise me, but she worked two jobs during most of my childhood years to make sure she had enough money to provide for us.

My role in our family was to do the best I could to be the best daughter. That meant getting good grades, always behaving, keeping comments and feelings to a minimum, and definitely no back talking. I was taught to be obedient and oblige others. Whatever needed to be done around the house, I had to help get it done. My aunt was in her late seventies when I was born, so I became her caregiver in her later years.

At the age of sixteen, I developed diabetes, and my aunt was dying of cancer. My mother was burning the candle at both ends, caregiving and still working more than twelve hours a day. Life was hard. Before my mother or anyone else knew it, I had become codependent. I thought my job in life was to help others, even at the cost of myself. I cried during most of my teenage and early-adult life. Caregiving felt like a bad dream that I couldn't get out of. I hated who I was but didn't know how to be anyone else. Not helping people felt selfish, even though helping others was the lead cause of my unhappiness and eventually my depression.

Codependency, in a nutshell, is a cluster of people-pleasing behavior patterns that a person picks up to survive a difficult childhood. Many codependents have parents/caregivers that struggle with mental health, substance use, alcohol addiction, and/or emotional regulation. This leaves the child to fend for themselves to survive in life. Subsequently, children learn to oblige the parent and avoid showing feelings or expressing needs as much as possible. If successful, the child creates a strategy to be in their parent's care without dealing with the emotional rollercoaster of emotions that generally all parents or caregivers of codependents have. It appears to be a great solution, until the child becomes an adult who only has people-pleasing skills to carry them through their life, leading them to say yes when they want to say no, feeling as if they must have all the answers to everyone's problems, and struggling to define who they are outside of the caregiver roles they have.

Some codependents even had to take care of their parents. I have worked with many clients who have reported helping their drunk parents into their bed at night, breaking up arguments between their parents/caregivers, helping with younger siblings, being responsible for meal prepping, cooking, cleaning, bathing, etc. These are things that no young child should be responsible for on a regular basis. This type of behavior snatches away the child's youth and throws them into adulthood. In some cases, the codependent is praised for putting others before themselves and will come to believe it is their job to do so. These thoughts are also carried out into adult life and can cause a codependent to feel they must take care of others. Whether we are at work, with friends, etc., we feel we must always be responsible for ourselves and everyone else around us.

You might be reading this, thinking to yourself how embedded codependent behavior patterns are in shaping who we are as people. And if so, you are correct. I'd spent the recent years of my life processing what this meant for me and finding ways to heal. I completed twelve-step groups, five years in therapy (on and off), spiritual coaching, and more. Yet still, I found myself feeling torn between the six-year-old who was trained to love and help everyone without questions and the thirty-five-year-old woman who was exhausted and eager to live her own life, discovering who she was and loving herself as God had made her, not because of her accomplishments or what she did for others.

This flight to see my dad was much different than my first, yet also similar in a lot of ways. I wasn't that six-year-old girl, eating snacks and looking at a movie, but I was still scared. What would it mean for me to have this conversation with my dad? How do you tell someone who thought they'd done a great job raising you that they actually didn't, and you're bitter, sad, disappointed, and confused about the way they have been treating you for the last thirty-five years? It sounded crazy just thinking about it. I couldn't even imagine saying it aloud to him.

As I gazed at the clouds and the huge buildings that looked like little squares in the sky, I heard the pilot speak over the intercom. "Hello, passengers. We have enjoyed this four-hour-and-forty-nine-minute flight with you. We have about forty minutes before we land. We ask that you relax, and we hope you enjoy your stay in Tampa, Florida."

I decided it might be best to take a little nap before I land and prepare myself to function as if nothing was wrong.

As we started to deboard the plane, I quickly gathered my purse. It felt like a good idea to call my best friend, Joanne. I was still somewhat upset with her for not spending my birthday with me in Las Vegas, especially since I was trying to relax before having this difficult conversation with my dad. Over the years, Joanne had regressed to her people-pleasing ways. She was 5'10" with long, curly hair, a caramel complexion, and a Coca-Cola bottle shape. Her wide hips always caught every man's attention everywhere we went. But for some reason, Joanne always gave her time to the first bum who asked for her phone number. And the cycle of emotional and verbal abuse would begin. First, they accused her of cheating; next, they asked her for money, then sex, and then they crossed all her boundaries. When the relationship was hanging on by a thread, Joanne would finally dump him and be single for about a month before the cycle started with a new man. She dated men who weren't on her level and complained to me about it constantly. When I mentioned returning to support groups or therapy, she accused me of not wanting to help her. I normally gave in and became her personal diary, but I had grown tired of our relationship being so one sided. I wanted to be able to share and get feedback too.

I decided to see if she could support me before I saw my dad. Even though Joanne had disappointed me many times before, I kept hoping that, one day, she would be the Joanne I met ten years ago, the one who helped me figure out life and what I needed.

I picked up the phone, found Joanne's number in the contacts, and dialed. "Hey, girl. I made it," I said with no enthusiasm when she picked up.

"Hey, sis! It's okay. It's not that bad; its only five days," she said, knowing I sounded down because I was in Tampa.

"Only five days … Yeah, okay," I said, laughing.

I started walking toward baggage claim and found a seat so I could continue talking to Joanne. "I've been thinking about writing a book, girl. Everything going on in my life is like a movie, and I'm the main character who doesn't know her lines."

"Book?" Joanne burst into laughter. "Taneshia, girl, please! You've been going to a few self-help summits and support groups at your church, and now you're an expert? Yeah, okay," she said nonchalantly.

I was hoping Joanne might be encouraging, but I had high hopes that weren't going to come true. She had a history of verbal abuse and would knock down any idea I shared to better myself unless she was included.

"Yeah, *I am* an expert!" I snapped. "I guess you forgot that I was trained as a facilitator for the twelve-step program at my church, completed the steps myself, then facilitated for four years. I've counseled families at my job for the last fifteen years; I have my master's degree in social work, and I've participated in my own therapy for five years. So, yeah, silly me for thinking I should write a book!"

"Okay, I know what that means. My apologies, Taneshia. Yes, you have done all of the above, not to mention the constant research you've done on codependency. Sorry, friend."

I was quiet for a few seconds, trying to calm down. "Thank you for saying that. *I have* done a lot! Anyway, girl, you know I'm out here with no support from my therapist at all. I haven't been able to get ahold of her. I've left like two messages now. What the hell? I'm in an emergency crisis with no support! I told her months ago I was going to make this trip to talk to my dad. You would think she would hit me back to give me some tips, encouragement, something!"

"Girl, she still ain't called?" Joanne said, sounding as shocked as I was.

"No. Last time I spoke with her, she was saying I was inconsistent with sessions, and I need to come every week if I really want help. I was thinking, damn, how crazy am I?" We both laughed.

"Well, girl, you do be trippin' sometimes," Joanne said in a matter-of-fact tone.

"Oh, let's not do that. 'Cause you know I got stories for days on you!" We chuckled again. "At any rate, I gotta go."

"So soon? Wait, I wanted to tell you what happened the other day! Girl, this man is crazy! Do you know we got into an argument about what kind of bread to buy?" Joanne said.

I was past done with hearing about Joanne and her crazy boyfriends. This one was an ex-con who had a job at a hardware store and drove his mama's car. He had three children that Joanne babysat like they were her own, and to top it off, there were rumors that he was dating other women. The fact that Joanne was with him made no sense to me. "Joanne, I can't believe that. I think it may be another indication that you guys aren't a good fit, sis. Fighting over bread? Come on now, girl! You deserve better."

"Better? Better like who, Ashton? He's screwing half the Bay Area. He takes off his drawers for any woman who looks half decent and is stupid enough to believe he's a good guy."

Ashton was my "friend" with whom I had started a "situationship" due to my lack of boundaries. He had multiple girlfriends, and I unwittingly became one of them. It didn't happen on purpose. Our bond just got closer and closer from us spending so much time together. The way Ashton held me made me feel things I hadn't felt in almost five years … since Shawn. It felt so good, I couldn't bear to let it go. I didn't feel ready. Nevertheless, this wasn't the first time I had tried to help Joanne, and instead of her hearing me, she criticized me. "Okay, let's just talk plain. You are referring to me, right? Being naïve enough to believe Ashton really cares about me, even though he has multiple women? I am aware of that. I am putting boundaries in place, Joanne."

"Boundaries? Kissing and rubbing are not boundaries. You think you're better than me just because you're not having sex. But you just wait. You'll see. Me and you are in the same situation, Taneshia, so don't talk to me about what I need to do. Focus on you!"

As I listened to Joanne disrespect me and become defensive, I realized she was right about one thing: I did need to focus on me. My dad was likely downstairs waiting on me, and I shouldn't have been wasting time with Joanne. What I thought was going to be a pep talk before I saw my dad had spiraled into another argument. It was time to let it go. "You know what, Joanne? You're right. I *do* need to focus on me. I have to go; my dad is downstairs. I'm not sure what you need to do in your situation. I've run out of ideas, but I trust you know what's best. I gotta go." I glanced at the phone one last time before I hit the end button.

"Taneshia?" Joanne said.

I hung up the phone. I wasn't going to listen to her foolishness when I was in the fight of my life, trying to figure out how to tell my dad I'd needed him to help me and guide me through the last thirty-five years of my life.

As I continued to follow the baggage claim signs, I remembered that my grandmother and my stepmom, Vanessa, had birthdays coming up while I was in town. *Damn, you can't show up empty handed, Taneshia*, I thought to myself. I saw a Body Shop store to the right of me as I walked toward baggage claim. "Oh, perfect. I'll stop here." I went inside the store and found two cute gift packages. I remembered my grandmother saying she liked the smell of mango, and I was hoping my stepmom did too. I grabbed two and placed them on the counter.

As I searched my purse for my credit card, I had flashes of the last time I saw my dad. It was about a year and a half prior. I had gotten upset while we were in Orlando and was crying during almost the entire ride back to Tampa. Seeing how my dad and stepmom lived always triggered me. We had stayed at their three-bedroom timeshare in Orlando. It had granite countertops, a huge patio with comfy chairs and a table, and luxury bedrooms with oversized TVs, couches, and bathrooms with marble flooring. With every glance across those rooms, I cried, thinking of the times my mother and I lived in a one-bedroom apartment with my aunt. It didn't seem fair that I was scraping by while my dad appeared to live high off the hog, unconcerned about the conditions my mother and I were living in. God had been good, and, over time, my mother purchased a home for us, but I still held resentment about his lack of support in my younger years.

As usual, it was another moment in my life when my dad didn't seem to care about me. Conjuring this memory reminded me of why I had to have this conversation with, not only my dad, but also the rest of my family. I needed to have a better understanding of where I fit in this family. I was hoping by showing them my love language, it would open the doors to them also loving me. I wanted to give loving them a try. I wanted to give my dad a try, to see if I could have the relationship I wanted with him if I was upfront and asked. I had made my mind up to tell him how I felt … for the moment.

The scary thing about healing that people don't talk enough about is the epiphanies. For the first time in my life, I was seeing my negative behavior patterns in my relationships, and I didn't like it. I was coming to terms with the fact that I was very rigid in my relationships with my family and everyone else, for that matter. People had to love me how I wanted it, when I wanted it; and if they didn't, that meant they didn't love me. And I treated them accordingly, avoiding them, blocking them, or being passive aggressive until they eventually left me alone. I didn't leave any room for people to love me how they wanted to, and I never advocated for myself or expressed my needs. In my opinion, showing needs was showing a weakness, and I wasn't going to be that vulnerable with anyone and risk getting hurt.

Reflecting on it now, I can see how the other person must've felt, never knowing how I felt but feeling the push back when they did or said something to hurt my feelings. It must've felt like a rollercoaster for my family and friends, and none of them deserved it. I was trying to use this trip to change that narrative about myself, starting with my father, stepmother, and grandmother. Giving my stepmother and grandmother gifts was something I had never done before. I was hoping it would create a space for me to grow a deeper relationship with both of them while showing them I love them.

I had gotten lost in my thoughts like I always do. I returned to reality when a soft voice asked me if I'd found everything okay. As she gave me the items in a cute bag, I smiled at her and walked out the door. One thing I hated about the Tampa airport was how big it is, but I managed to find the air trans train before it got too crowded and boarded with everyone else.

I heard my phone ring. I looked down and saw that it was my dad. "Hey, Dad. I'm almost there. I'm on the train to baggage claim now."

"Hello, baby. Okay, perfect! Listen, I'm going to head over now. Go ahead and get your bags from baggage claim, and I'll meet you at the escalator."

"Okay, sounds good," I said with a smile. I always hoped that if I had a smile on my face, people would genuinely hear happiness in my voice.

I got off the train and followed the crowd to baggage claim, hoping I wouldn't have to wait forever for my things. As the bell sounded on the luggage belt, the bags began coming in. One by one, everyone took their bags from the carousel. I saw my orange suitcase coming down the lane and was eager to grab it. I pulled it from the carousel and started looking for the handlebar to pull it down the escalator. As I started my way down the escalator, I saw my dad smiling and waving. Even though I had plans to come to him as a grown woman in need of answers and apologies, I found myself reverting to that little girl who was shy and scared of the thought of asking her father for any more than what he was giving. Thoughts of my dad not loving me or not talking to me anymore if I asked for more of him overshadowed my original plans, so I took a deep breath and put a big smile on my face while waving back at him. Deep down inside, I was happy to see him; I just didn't know how to express to him that I needed him to be a father. How do you tell someone who thinks they're doing a great job that you feel like they aren't? And, most importantly, how do you bring it up after thirty-five years of saying nothing? It felt redundant and unimportant. I almost felt selfish for bringing this up in his golden years. Thoughts flooded my mind, but as usual, by the time I got down the escalator, all I said was "Hi, Daddy."

"Is that my daughter, Taneshia Johnson? How are you doing?" he said with a huge grin.

As he wrapped his arms around me, I felt my body freeze. Part of me craved his touch and part of me was so angry that I wanted to push him away. *Do you really think a big hug is going to make everything better? I need you to pick me up from school, give me money to shop with my friends, help with my homework, and protect me from people who pick on me and call me names. I need a father!* But I was coming to the realization that those moments were long gone for me. I wasn't five or fifteen anymore. I was thirty-five. God and I had done a good job of taking care of me when my dad didn't. So

I found myself embracing the side of me that wanted his affection and love and ignoring the other side that was angry and bitter about what I'd endured as a child.

Therapy was pulling out emotions in me that I'd hidden for decades. I didn't know what to do with them. I didn't have a chance to connect with Dr. Jones before I left to see him, so I had to figure out what to do on my own. She and I had talked about me sharing my feelings with him, but she didn't give much instruction on how. I loved Dr. Jones as my therapist and member of my support system, but lately, she wasn't giving much direction. I didn't know if I was expecting too much from her. Maybe it was my job to figure out how to express my feelings to people. I was getting more comfortable with expressing my feelings in the heat of the moment, but bringing up certain topics outside of conflict still felt awkward to me.

I got out of my thoughts, let my luggage fall to the side, and grabbed my father with both hands, wrapping them around his waist. I softly said, "It's so good to see you, Dad." We stood there for about a minute, just enjoying the ability to hold each other and see each other face to face, not via phone.

"You only got one bag this time," he said.

We laughed. "Yes, only one," I said with a chuckle.

"It's a big one, though," he said, his voice straining from picking up my suitcase.

"Dad, it has a pull thingy on the side," I said, pointing to my luggage.

"Oh, praise God. Your old dad's not as strong as he used to be, Taneshia. Can you believe I'm seventy-two? Wow, I didn't think I would get this old."

"Dad, you always say that." We laughed again.

As we boarded the elevator to the garage, I could feel my dad looking at me. He always did that. Part of me always felt like I had to look perfect, dress perfect, *be perfect.* I never knew what those feelings were about, but I was learning that I was too hard on myself. For the first time, I decided to look at my dad and say something. "What?" I said with a confused expression.

"Nothing, just looking at how beautiful you are, baby," he said, embracing me with his arms around my shoulders.

Beautiful … He thinks I'm beautiful. Then why weren't you around when I was little? How come I only saw you during the summer? No phone calls or anything?

As we waited for the elevator to approach our floor, we held hands. I felt confused. My dad was saying all the right things, but they didn't add up to my memories. For a moment, I still felt like the girl who had met her father for the first time, holding his hand through the parking garage. The feeling was so powerful that it brought a few tears to my eyes. There we were again, holding hands and smiling at each other.

Looking at my relationship with my dad from a healed place, I could see clearly that he really did love me. Finally, my dad was meeting my need to be seen and cherished by him. I was happy. I felt like this trip might be different. Maybe this trip wasn't the best for bringing up anything, especially since I hadn't gotten a chance to follow up with Dr. Jones. Maybe I would just enjoy my dad. Maybe it was all in my mind, and I was being rigid with my dad, not allowing him to love me how he wanted. Maybe this was his version of love. We held hands and smiled at each other during the entire walk to the car. I didn't know what was happening, but I knew that, for once, I felt special and important to my father, and it was priceless.

HEALING IS...

CRYING OFTEN

UNLEARNING BEHAVIOR PATTERNS

Watching your relationships with others change

Feeling confused

Being your own best friend

WWW.TJSELFCARE.COM

2

Feel It, Process It, Let It Go

I was exhausted. My plane came in late, and there was nothing left to do but rest. As soon as I hit the bed, I fell asleep. Luckily, I managed to remember that the next day was Saturday, and I would be going to church with my dad and grandmother. My dad's side of the family were Seventh-Day Adventist. I wasn't, but I still respected their beliefs every summer I came to visit.

The next morning, Dad and I were on our way to church. The dress I'd laid out, to my surprise, fit beautifully and didn't even need to be ironed. As we were getting ready to leave, my step-mom stopped me. "Taneshia, look at you! You look so beautiful. I like that dress," she said, embracing my shoulder with a look of admiration.

"I like this one too. I was hoping it would fit." I turned to the left and saw my dad walking toward the door.

"Okay, daughter, are you ready to go? I love that dress, Taneshia!"

"Thank you, Dad," I said.

"Okay, dear, we're leaving," my dad said, giving my stepmom a kiss.

As I watched them kiss, it made me reflect on their relationship. They had been together for twenty-one years. A memory came across my mind that I tried to avoid, but it kept pressing. I remembered I'd learned about their wedding after it had already happened.

The first time I heard from my stepmom was in 1997, when my dad was in a bad car accident. I was supposed to come down for the summer. She called to inform me that my dad was hit by a twelve-wheeler truck on his way to Alabama and had been in the hospital for about a week already, prior to anyone calling me. Little did I know, they were already engaged and got married in January of 1998. I couldn't believe it.

I didn't understand what it was with my dad. Did he not think I would want to go to family events? Did they not care? Or were they just unorganized and didn't think about me at all? I had brought this issue up to my dad in the past. His response was that he was broke and didn't have any money for me to fly down. In the past, I had accepted his responses with a grudge, still feeling like he should have found a way to make it happen so I could be there too and be a part of the family.

All these memories made me feel indifferent about my decision not to say anything. I could hear my therapist in my ear saying, "Taneshia, advocating for yourself is about you, not others." So who cares if he was old; he was still my dad. He still owed me some form of an explanation.

Suddenly, I felt something. I snapped out of my daze to find my dad standing next to me with his hand on my shoulder. "Ready, dear?" he said.

As usual, I put on a big fake grin and said, "Yeah, let's go. Bye, Vanessa."

"Okay, sweetie, bye bye," she said.

As my dad opened the passenger car door, I smiled at him. "Thank you, Daddy."

"Of course, of course. Let's roll, daughter!"

As my dad walked over to the driver side, I noticed he moved a little slower than he did when I was younger. It was funny how I saw myself getting older but never realized my dad was getting older too. He opened his car door and slowly lowered his body onto the seat. He placed one leg in first, then the other leg. "Ugh ..." he grunted. "Taneshia, ooh wee, let me tell you, getting older is no joke. I praise God for every day."

"Amen, Dad. I hear you. I'm glad you're still here." I reached over, giving him a hug, holding back tears because the little girl in me wanted me to advocate for the father I always wanted, but the grown woman version of me saw so many signs that made me feel guilty; and it felt like it wasn't the right time.

As we pulled out of the driveway, my dad asked me my favorite question. "So, daughter, where do you wanna go eat breakfast? I know last night, we laughed about Waffle House, but there are other places," he said.

"You know the place I love," I said.

We both laughed. "You wanna go to the Waffle House."

"Yes, sir," I said, dancing in my seat, thinking about eating that waffle.

"Okay, let's go," he said with a chuckle.

We started on our way to Waffle House. I began reflecting again about not being a part of my dad and stepmom's wedding. I was learning to ask myself why certain events were important to me. Why did that event stand out? And was there something I needed to know so I could resolve my feelings? Most of the time, I felt crazy, assessing every situation, going back and forth about things and how it made me feel. But it was helpful, and it was part of my healing work. For too long, as a child and an adult, I minimized my experiences and how they made me feel. I never took the time to understand how I felt. In this case, I needed my dad to explain to me why he made me feel unloved or uncared for by him. I had never asked these questions before, but I needed to know now, to process my feelings and move on.

How could you not make sure your own daughter was in your wedding? The only conclusion I came up with in my mind was that I was not good enough to attend. I was "the outside child" whose birth had ruined his perfect family. I must've been a reminder of a bad mistake my father and his family wish never happened. That had to be the reason. But through therapy, I was learning not to jump to assumptions. I must allow people to explain their side. It was not my job to make summarizations and excuses for people. It was my job to hold others accountable for their behavior.

Our job as recovering people pleasers and codependents is to find evidence to deny the negative thoughts in our heads. In this case, my thoughts were telling me neither my father nor his side of the family loved me. All the evidence I could remember pointed to those feelings being correct. I wanted to be loved by them. As a child, I didn't have words to express my feelings, so I tried to get love through good behavior and accomplishments …

still nothing. Now, as an adult, I was trying my best to reach out, and it *still* wasn't working.

I sat in the car, occasionally glancing at my dad as he stared back at me with a look of endearment. I smiled at him and continued to look out the window, trying to figure out what I was doing wrong with him and his side of the family. One thought came to mind, and that was to speak my needs. I could hear Dr. Jones' voice in my head, saying, "Taneshia, it is your job to tell others what you need. Communicate your feelings. They deserve to be heard." But what she didn't seem to understand was that my only feeling was anger, and the only words that seemed to come easily to me were spelled with four letters and were not pleasant.

My anger scared me because I thought I would lose friends and family if people really knew how I felt about how they treated me. I had successfully bottled up my emotions for as long as I could. However, I was learning that I had to let that coping mechanism go because it was no longer serving me. My internal anger had burned my insides to a crisp and left me depressed, confused, and hopeless.

I was determined to tell my dad how I felt while at breakfast. The thoughts that told me I don't need my dad were lies. I would often think to myself, *There's no need to have a relationship with him, and if there is, why bring up old thoughts and feelings?* I figured that with therapy and time I would get over the painful truth on my own. No need to resolve things with my parents at all. I could do it by myself. I was convinced that the only being that truly wanted me to be here was God. God gave me a gift to be able to empathize with people and nurture them, and that's what I was doing. I had no idea that state of thought was the grounds for my depression. I didn't know how to be who I was because I despised my own existence; it just seemed to bring so much sadness to people around me. And in my mind, that sadness was preventing people from loving me. What I didn't realize was that it was inevitably preventing *me* from loving myself as well.

While deep in thought, I saw that Dad and I had made it to Waffle House. We parked the car, walked into the restaurant, and ordered our food. My dad sat on one side and I on the other. He looked at me, holding my hand while sipping his coffee. At that moment I felt important to him and decided to start the conversation while I had the courage. I figured I should start off by asking him how he was doing before diving in with "Why don't you love me?!"

"So, how have you been, Dad? What's new?"

"Well, not much. Just kicking around, doing the same thing, managing the rental property, running errands, and doing Uber on the side. I get up early, around six a.m. every day, so I work for about three hours until Vanessa gets up. Then I grab us breakfast, we eat, I run some errands, and then, before you know it, it's nine p.m., and I'm headed to bed, dear." My dad chuckled. "Taneshia, this is life at seventy-two."

I gave him a matter-of-fact look and nodded. "Hey, it sounds amazing to me, Dad. You've earned it." Although I'd said he earned it with my mouth, I wondered if I really believed that. And if I did, how could I feel cheated by him for so many years?

As I ate with my father, I glanced occasionally at his hands. When I was six years old, I was amazed that we had the same hands, and I still was. His hands were like mine—long, with oval-shaped fingers. I watched him eat his omelet. His beard was gray now and under his eyes were small wrinkles. This was my father, the same man whom I'd watched build a business, climb ladders, wash windows, and do estimates all day. Taking life one day at a time with no clue that his daughter was suffering and needed him. But whose fault was that? Was I blaming my father for something he wasn't aware of, expecting him to know what I needed? I was confused about the direction in which I should go. During almost the entire plane ride, I had been thinking of this moment, and now that it was here, I was stuck.

My dad and I sat in silence as we ate. Occasionally, he reached over and ate a bite of my waffle. I smiled as I watched him chomp away. He didn't believe in leaving any food behind. That made me think of myself. I started to notice all the characteristics he and I shared, even though we lived far from each other. I took the last sip of my coffee, looked at him, and reflected on memories of him and me.

"Okay, Ms. Johnson, are you ready?" he said.

"Yep, I am."

As we were wrapping up our breakfast, the waitress came back with the check. "Thank you, ma'am," my dad said, taking the bill.

I grabbed my dad's hand. "Dad, if you don't mind, I'd like to treat you to breakfast," I said, pulling out my credit card and holding back tears. *Look at everything he's doing for me …* Was it that he was a bad father, or did he do the best he could, considering the circumstances? It couldn't have been easy trying to coparent with someone who lived on the other side of the country, but I couldn't make excuses for my dad. He was responsible for his actions, regardless. I had to focus on my needs. I had hoped I would get the courage to say something during breakfast, but as we both took our last bites, I decided to let it go for now. Based on the thoughts in my head, I could tell I wasn't clear about how I wanted to bring this up with him.

I looked off to the side and thought, *Taneshia, you've got four more days to say something.*

"Okay, dear. Well, thank you."

"You're welcome, Daddy," I said.

We held hands for a few seconds, smiling at each other. My dad grabbed his wallet, and I gathered my purse and sweater from the table. "Here you go, sweetie. You guys have a great day," the waitress said while returning my credit card.

My dad and I walked out of the restaurant. He opened the door for me, and we walked toward the car. He turned on a Christian radio station, and I heard one of my favorite songs by Tasha Cobbs, "He Knows My Name." That song always took me to a place of love, peace, and belonging. l closed my eyes and sang the lyrics to myself, reflecting on how God walks with me, how He talks with me and tells me I'm His own. The tears I'd done such a good job at holding back were now falling down my face and landing on my dress. I looked for tissue in my purse while glancing at my dad. He was singing along, moving his hands to the melody. I stared at him in silence. He didn't even know I was crying because I didn't feel like he really loved me. As my father here on earth, his job was to love me; yet the only love I felt was from my Father in heaven. The song reminded me that no matter how I felt here on earth, God did love me, and He was my *real* Father anyway. I quickly looked away and continued to wipe my tears and nose with tissue. Before I knew it, we were pulling up to the church parking lot.

I remembered coming to this church many times as a child. The story was that members of my family were some of the founding members. It was a white church with an off-white door. It looked small outside, but it was huge inside. As the car's tires crunched through the dirt and rocks of the gravel parking lot, I pulled the passenger mirror down and retrieved lip gloss from my purse, smearing some on my lips. I checked my hair and sprayed mist on my face. My eyes were slightly red from crying.

I straightened my glasses and cleared my throat. "Wow, here we are! Same church," I said, trying not to sound too sad about it.

"Yep, yep, same church. Mama is already here. I told some people you were coming, so they may look for you," he said.

People at my dad's church always made me wonder. They would say things like, "Oh, you're here this summer … So good to see you!" or "You look just like your dad. Look how you have grown." I often wondered what they'd heard about me and my existence and what they thought about it. Until my therapist brought it to my attention, I didn't even realize the relationship I had with my dad wasn't normal. I was already in my twenties before I started wondering why my dad didn't live in California with my mom and me. I had always spent the summers with my dad and didn't see or hear from him much during the year. I assumed that was what the relationship was supposed to look like. Having a father who picked me up from school, helped with homework, and taught me how to drive were things I had dreamed about, but I let those thoughts go when I realized the distance between us. I also often wondered if my dad would even want to do those things with me. If he did, why did he choose to live so far away? I was learning I had missed out on the relationship I wanted with my dad out of fear that he didn't want to experience those things with me. As a child, I was too afraid to ask, and as an adult, I didn't want to deal with the rejection if his response was negative. In this moment, I could see how my assumptions and fears of being rejected may have caused me to miss out on the relationship I always wanted and never knew I needed.

We both got out of the car and headed to the church. My dad walked beside me and eventually ahead of me. He opened the door for me, and we walked in. I could smell the fresh scent of gardenia and sweet pea from the flowers in the lobby. My dad led the way to a pew behind my grandmother. As he patted her back, she turned around and waved at us, making sure to look at me and smile. She whispered "Hello" to him and placed her hand in mine. "Hey, baby," she said.

"Hi, Grandma," I said, holding her hand a little tighter. I was genuinely happy to see her again and be there to celebrate her birthday.

The rest of the congregation was singing a song from the hymn book called "Glory to God." I glanced up at the screen above the pulpit, placed my purse on my lap, and looked for page 655 in my own hymn book.

I felt my phone vibrating, so I picked up my purse and fished through it. I found my phone and saw that I had a missed call from Ashton and a missed text message from my co-worker Lisa that read: Hey, girl! Hope your vacay is great and time with your dad is amazing. They've created new reports for us when you get back. Let me know if you need help.

I appreciated Lisa for letting me know, but considering I still had four more days with my dad and eight more days before I had to go back to that hell I called a job, this was not the time. I grew angry as I read the text, angry that my life had equated to a job I hated and angry that I felt stuck in a field of work I no longer had a desire to do. I loved social work, but I wanted to find another way to help people. I was unsure of the direction in which my life was going. I had gained weight over the last five years; my diabetes wasn't under control, and there was still no man or baby in my near future … not that I could see. I was fully aware of the foolishness I was involved in with Ashton, and I hated myself for it. I tried to focus back on the worship service, but I was already frustrated.

A text message popped up from Ashton while my phone was still in my hand: Hi, baby. How is your vacation? I miss you. I can't wait to hear your voice. Can I call you later?

I rolled my eyes. *See me for what?!* I thought. I was just another woman on his list. Why did he want to hear from me?

I turned my attention back to the service. To my surprise, I had dazed through the entire song-singing portion, and the minister was now giving his sermon. He preached from the book of James. I looked at my dad, and he pointed to the scripture in his Bible. I pulled mine out and turned to James 1:2-4. It read, "Consider it pure joy, my brothers and sisters, whenever you face trials of many kinds, because you know that the testing of your faith produces perseverance."

As I read the scripture, I phased out into my thoughts again. Was I being tested by my faith? I knew God was aware of my pain, but sometimes I wondered why He wouldn't take the pain away. Why did I have to endure it? I felt like it was breaking me at my core, and I had done everything I could to fix it. I was in therapy; I had participated in the Celebrate Recovery program for five years; I still facilitated a group every Friday night at my church. Didn't God see I was trying? I had faith, but sheesh! When was He going to kick in? I was angry at Him, even though I didn't want to admit it. I almost felt too unworthy to admit it. He was God, Jehovah, my Lord and Savior, my everything, the only thing I had left that loved me. I knew for a fact that when I came into this world, He was there. When I was in the hospital being diagnosed with diabetes, there were nights when I just lay in my bed and cried. I was alone, lonely, and scared. But the one thing I knew was consistent was God. I did count my trials as joy. I felt my whole life was a trial. I needed God to step in and show me if I should have this conversation with my dad.

Is it too late?

There is an old saying that goes "Stir up old stuff, and it will stink." Was this old stuff? And if so, would I be able to tolerate the smell? Or maybe it had always smelled, and I had been masking it with fake smiles, fancy hair, degrees, and jobs I didn't even want anymore.

I got lost in thought longer than I wanted to and missed the sermon. I felt my dad's arm on my shoulder and people looking at me, their faces full of delight, eager to speak to me. "Hi, Taneshia! It's so good to see you. Look at you, looking just like your dad." That was the line I heard repeatedly for thirty minutes, until we walked out of the church.

My dad managed to hold my hand the entire time as we walked through the crowd, and I embraced him. It made me want to just bask in the moment and be thankful for the time I had. After tossing back and forth, I had made up my mind. I wasn't going to say anything during this trip. If my therapist asked, I would just tell her it wasn't a good time. I could see I now had the relationship I'd wanted with my dad for so long. I just had to spend more time with him building it.

"All right!" my dad said, throwing up his hand, waving good-bye to his friends. "Let's go, daughter. We have to get ready for your grandmother's birthday dinner."

"Oh, is that tonight?" I said, surprised.

"Yep, you picked a great time to come."

"Yeah … great," I said with pause. I had hoped I could give her the gift I'd bought in private, maybe even use it to open a conversation with her. Since dinner had turned into a big family event, I figured maybe going to her house beforehand would be easier. "Hey, Dad, maybe I could go back to Grandma's house and meet you all for dinner. Is Aunt Susan going too?"

"Yeah, yeah, she is. Okay. You wanna spend some time with them? No problem," he said, giving me another hug from the side. "I'll see you at the restaurant, baby. Let me go get Mother. Your aunt Susan just pulled up," he said, pointing to her car.

My aunt Susan was a beautiful chocolate-toned woman. She stood 5'9", with big brown eyes and flowy black, curly hair. She got out of her car and came toward me. "Hey, girl! How are you?" she said, giving me a big hug.

"I'm doing well," I said, extending my arms to hug her back. "I'm going with you and Grandma back to the house. I was hoping we could relax and talk."

"Oh yeah, that would be great. You know we're celebrating Mother's birthday, so we can all go to the restaurant together," she said happily.

"Okay, great. I'll get Grandma from the church," I said.

"Okay, I'll come with you. She may need some help walking through the crowd."

My aunt and I walked back into the church, but she got caught up talking to church members. I continued to the sanctuary, where I knew Grandma and my dad were. My dad had already helped her get up and my grandma was making her way through the crowd. As people stared at me, I continued toward her. I didn't feel like holding conversations with more people I didn't know. The possible thoughts they had of me gave me too much anxiety.

"Oh, you didn't have to come in, baby; I got her. I'm helping Mother to the car now," my dad said, rubbing my shoulder. I smiled, this time sincerely. I liked when my dad called me endearing names like "baby" or "honey," and his favorite, "black princess."

As all three of us got closer to the exit, I saw my aunt still at the front, laughing and talking with some of the church people. I looked at all of us together … We were like a family. The only difference was that I could also see how everyone was much older. It made me reflect on the years I had wasted being unhappy and not getting my needs met, convincing myself that my dad and his family didn't care about me. Even thinking about it made me sad because, deep down, I knew it wasn't true. I was irritated by my own thoughts. This man had made it a point to spend quality time with me since I was six years old. I saw him every summer. Not to mention, from the time I turned eighteen, I talked to my dad every week. He even sent me money while I was in college once a month and helped me pay for my car. How could I even think that about him?

My thoughts were disrupted by my dad calling my name. "Taneshia, take your grandmother's bag," he said, handing it to me.

"Okay," I said as I took the bag and tossed it in the back seat.

My dad folded my grandmother's walker and gave it to me to put in the back seat as well. As I got in, my aunt started the car, and we were on our way to my grandma's house for lunch and, likely for them, a nap before her birthday celebration.

We arrived at the house, and my aunt parked the car. As she got out, she asked me to help Grandma into the house. I pulled out the walker and started having thoughts. I reflected on the many times I had laid in my bed at night, wishing I'd gotten a call from her as a child, asking me how I was doing. What was new with me. What was my favorite song. When I came down for the summer, where were my moments of baking cookies with my grandmother or learning her recipes.

I soon realized that perhaps I wasn't sad about her but about the idea of her and the things I wanted to do. Growing up, the only grandmother I had a relationship with was my mom's mother, Grandma Fannie. With Grandma Fannie, summers were filled with her baking me biscuits and laughing at me being afraid of lightning bugs and rabbits that hopped in her yard. Summers were so fun with her. I helped her plant tomatoes, carrots, and other vegetables in her garden. Growing up in the city, I had never seen such huge backyards before. My grandma's yard covered at least 1200 square feet. Her little three-bedroom white house sat right in the middle. During my first summer there, I was amazed to see orange dirt for the first time. I wrote my name in it all over the yard. My cousins and I ate popsicles in the backyard, laughing and playing until the sun went down, and Grandma would call us in for dinner. It really was like something people see on TV.

My grandmother couldn't read or write, but one thing she did do well was show me love. When I was born, she flew from Georgia to California at seventy-seven years old to see me. She made it a point to get to know who I was and build a relationship with me, and she asked my mother to send me to her during the summer. She worked at a hamburger joint in her city and used to bring me home freshly made hamburgers and fries at least once a week.

A bright yellow taxi would pull up into the yard, and I'd

eagerly sit outside, waiting for her. Even though I loved her hamburgers, I was really waiting for a hug. I'd run up to her, and she would laugh with open arms. We looked in each other's eyes, and then she'd give me a big kiss on my forehand. Soon after, she'd pull my hamburger from her purse. Grandma Fannie was my example of how a grandmother and her grandchild should be.

My maternal grandmother was a place of refuge. I always knew I would be loved and consoled by her. Grandma Fannie passed away when I was nineteen years old. It was one of the saddest days in my life. I wasn't sure whether people loved me or if they loved what I did for them, but with Grandma Fannie, I knew it was me. She loved Taneshia—shy, goofy, fun, kind-spirited Taneshia. I didn't have to do anything but show up and be loved by her. That was the love I was missing with my dad's mother. It didn't seem like she cared; or perhaps she was leaving it up to me to establish a relationship with her. It was confusing, and most of the time, I avoided interacting with her because I didn't understand her love language. I'd call her, and we'd talk for about five minutes, then that was it. No "I love you" to end the call or anything. With Grandma Fannie, I'd hear "Grandma love her baby" or "Love my Taneshia" multiple times during one phone call. Part of me died when Grandma Fannie passed, and I secretly told myself I had no grandmother. Because it really felt like I didn't.

Healing work is just that—work. I was learning I couldn't profess to be healing and growing while still carrying ill feelings toward people in my heart. It was my job to advocate for my needs and express them to people I cared for; try to find the common ground. In relationships, we must remember that our perspective and the perspectives of the other people involved all must be accounted for. I was telling myself my grandmother didn't love me and making decisions based on assumptions I had created in my mind. The goal during this trip was to come to an understanding about who she was, to observe her and make conclusions based on her actions, not how I felt about her.

The way we feel is valid. And in this case, I had an obligation to attempt to understand her, give her an opportunity to explain her side and explain her love language. One thing my paternal grandmother did was send me gifts every year for my birthday. Perhaps she wasn't as openly expressive with her love as Grandma Fannie was. I was open to exploring all these things with her, no longer treating her based on assumptions and feelings of rejection I'd carried in my heart.

As she and I walked toward the house, she gave me her key. I opened the door, and we both went inside. My aunt had gotten my grandmother a small kitten that I watched hop from one side of the couch to the other. She was adorable, and to my surprise, I wasn't scared. I sat on the couch and placed my bags down.

"Go ahead and make yourself at home, Taneshia," my grandma said. Your aunt Susan already made lunch. It's on the stove. When she comes in, we'll eat."

"Okay, sounds good. You need some help with anything, Grandma?"

"No, I'm fine. I'm going to wash up before supper."

"Okay." Even though I wanted to go in her room with her and keep talking, I felt like I might be disturbing her and her time to unwind before dinner. Instead, I lay on the couch and started drifting off to sleep.

I felt someone touching my leg. I woke up to see it was my aunt. "Taneshia, why don't you take a little nap? I'll leave a plate in the kitchen for you if you wake up and get hungry. We have about three hours before we go to dinner.

"Okay. Thanks, Aunt Susan," I said, taking my shoes off and getting more comfortable. As soon as I found a small blanket to throw across my legs, my grandmother's kitten came over. I picked her up and pet her. She purred while stretching her tiny paws up toward me. I held her a little closer then placed her beside me and pet her while I drifted back to sleep. I heard my phone vibrating and felt the kitten jump on my thighs and climb down to get it. She and I were competing, trying to get to my phone before it stopped buzzing.

It was Joanne. "Hey, girl. How is it going? I know this is day two. You sure you gonna stay the full five days?" she said when I answered. I could hear the smirk in her tone.

"I don't know, girl. It's a lot. My thoughts are taking me out, girl!" I said, whispering so my aunt and grandmother wouldn't hear me.

"What's wrong? You're gonna tell him, right, Taneshia? Girl, you better! You're thirty-five years old, Taneshia! Don't hold on to all this pain and shit! Tell people how you feel!"

"Joanne, I love you, but sometimes I just need you to listen, sis. I'm doing the best I can. It's hard enough just being down here, not to mention also trying to spend time with other family members. My inner child is crying and dying inside, girl, every minute I'm here. She wants to leave. She is me. I wanna leave!" I was getting emotional and struggling to communicate. "Listen, girl, I gotta go. I'll call back."

"Okay, sis. And Taneshia … thank you for explaining. I'm really sorry. Take the time you need, girl. I didn't realize how hard this was for you."

"Thank you," I said, crying. My tears had rolled from my eyelids to my mouth, and I could taste the salty flavor. I hung up, lay on my side, and cried.

As my body shook and my throat grew tight, I just let the tears fall. I felt my grandma's kitten jump back on me. It was as if she knew I was sad. She lay on my legs, looking at me. I turned back around toward the window, looking at the birds flying past, wishing I was one of them and could fly away. I had changed my mind about having these hard conversations. Healing felt like too much work that I wasn't prepared to do. All it seemed to do was cause feelings of sadness and pain.

I couldn't believe all of this was happening in my life. Where was my happy ending? All those books I'd read about self-care, self-love, and healing from codependency talked about things finally getting better for those who did the work. The authors explained that those who did the work would see the fruit of their labor and bask in the peace and joy they had learned to cultivate in their own lives. Where was mine? Was I not doing the work? Every day, I set boundaries, telling people how I felt, learning to not jump to conclusions and allow my heart to be my guide instead of the thoughts of others. All of this was work, so why was I going through so many hardships? I didn't think healing was supposed to look like this. I felt cheated by God and life. It was as if all my hard work was just resulting in more pain.

Nevertheless, I was committed to my healing journey. I had to feel it, process it, and let it go. Here I was, petting my grandmother's cat, sitting on the couch, crying, when I should've been getting up and going into her room to talk. But I didn't know what to say. Parts of me didn't feel prepared. Maybe confronting my dad and grandmother was too much for one trip. I was having second thoughts and regretting even deciding to come down and visit. I just felt confused and broken inside, with no idea of how to feel better.

I got up and heard my aunt laughing with someone on the phone. I walked to my grandma's room and saw her napping with the TV on. I stood there, looking at her while my thoughts taunted me. *Damn Taneshia, you missed your opportunity. Your aunt is on the phone, and your grandma is asleep. You were supposed to go to them and finally tell them how you feel. Let them know you want to build a relationship with them and get to know them. Tell them you love them because they are family, and you want to love them for who they are. Be an adult for once! You help your clients begin conversations with family and friends all the time; yet you can't seem to do it for your-self. Just go in there, lightly wake her up, and say, "Hey, Grandma. I love you, and I want us to be closer." That's it! Easy! She loves you. Of course, she's going to say okay.*

My thoughts were so sure … but I wasn't. I looked down and walked away, wiping tears from my face. Even though I had tried my best to come here as Adult Taneshia, Little Taneshia was here and in full form. My inner child was convinced she would be rejected. And the best thing to do was play with my grandma's cat and nap until we went to dinner. I had tried so hard to make "grown woman" moves by telling my dad I wanted to spend time with my grandma. I even helped out and tried to be in good spirits. Yet, I just couldn't do it. I felt like I was projecting my needs and feelings onto other people. What if she told me she didn't understand what I was talking about? Then I would have to explain everything from the beginning, starting with "Why don't you have pictures of me as a child?" all the way to "You don't seem to love me like you love everyone else." Or worse, what if I hurt her feelings by sharing with her that I didn't feel like we had a relationship? She might've thought we did! Then I would have to apologize to her, and things would be awkward. I even questioned if it was a conversation that needed to be had or if there were just action steps I needed to take to get to know her better, like calling more and sending gifts. Maybe this one-on-one come-to-Jesus moment I'd had in my head wasn't necessary. I hadn't talked to my therapist about speaking with my grandmother either, so I was completely making up this entire intervention on my own. I had felt so compelled to do this when I was on the plane, but now I just felt insecure and silly.

I slowly headed back to the couch. Crying, I threw the blanket back over me and reached for my grandma's cat.

I slept longer than anticipated and woke up to my dad touching me on the shoulder. "Taneshia, we're gonna go to dinner tomorrow instead of today. I came to pick you up. Did you eat already?"

"No, but it's OK. I'm fine," I said as if coming out of a daze. My grandma's cat was still on my side, napping peacefully.

To my surprise, my grandma was sitting beside me, watching TV. "I didn't wanna wake you. You and Princess were sleeping so peacefully, girl," she said.

"Oh, that's her name, Princess ..." I called her name and the kitten woke up and came closer. Her eyes were so warm and endearing. I pet her softly. I was searching for that look in my grandma and dad's eyes as a sign that it was okay to express how I felt, but it seemed like I was never going to see it. It was up to me to bring up the conversation and express how I felt, and I just couldn't do it. My fear of rejection was too strong.

My grandma patted me on my leg. I gave her a hug and lay on

her shoulder for a few moments while she and my dad talked. She grabbed my hand and held it, and I felt warm tears emerge from my eyes. I quickly wiped them before she or my dad saw. I was so confused. She was showing love to me for the first time that I could remember. I sat there, quietly holding her hand, trying to remember other times that maybe I had forgotten about.

A few thoughts came to my mind. *Remember, when you were really sick that summer and had a sore throat? And she made you some honey with tea and made you drink water with a small piece of charcoal in it. You thought she was crazy, but you lay down on this same couch and felt better. Remember when you went with her for a church function and helped her out at the library? You forgot all those times? Now look … she's holding your hand. Maybe she does love you. Maybe there is no need for a conversation. Maybe it's you, Taneshia!*

I sat there, processing my thoughts, wondering if it was me. Maybe *she did* love me. Parts of me knew for sure that she did because I was her grandchild. But other parts doubted it because we didn't have much of a relationship. But there could be love without a relationship, right?

I saw my dad and grandmother's lips moving as they both looked at me seemingly in awe as if they were looking at a beautiful painting or mural. I figured it was time to get out of my head and probably say something. I smiled and nodded. "Yeah," I said, laughing, hoping I was on key with whatever they were talking about and didn't have to actually say words. I was too caught up in my own thoughts to participate in their conversation. I looked down at my hand to see that Grandma was still holding it. Princess and I looked at each other. It was almost like she knew how loving and caring my grandmother was and wanted me to realize it too. After a while, Princess got jealous and climbed on the couch between us. She reached out for my grandmother, and my grandmother let go of my hand while I sat there, laughing.

Even though I didn't have the conversation with her, I began to feel the same type of love from her that I'd felt from Grandma Fannie. I wondered about my assumptions and remembered that my grandmother was eighty-eight years old. She and Grandma Fannie had come from the Jim Crow era, when Black people were told they were free but still weren't given a lot of rights. And particularly, Black women were not taught to express themselves or even think it was okay to do so. I wondered if I was assuming she was this strong Black woman who felt comfortable expressing her feelings but just didn't care about me, or was she just a woman who wasn't used to expressing her feelings, and I was taking it personal as if she was only this way with me.

I conjured up memories and began to realize she was like this with everyone. The difference was that other family members, who I knew had a relationship with her, called her, brought up conversations with her, and, most importantly, they assumed they were loved and that she cared. That's something I was still working on, not just with her and my dad, but everyone in my life. I was kind of happy we weren't going to dinner and the day was over. I was learning I had a lot to figure out for myself before having a conversation with my grandmother, and maybe even my dad.

3

Coffee, Conversations, and Tears

The sound of the alarm clock jolted me from my sleep. I hit the clock and glanced at the time. It was five a.m. "Ugh," I grunted, stretching my hands up toward the ceiling. "Thank you, Jesus, for another day. Day three …" I said, getting up from the bed.

I took my clothes off from the night before, amazed I had slept in them. That was a first in a while. It was an indication of how tired and emotionally drained I was. I grabbed my towel and shower cap and walked toward the shower. I opened the door, careful not to wake my stepmom and dad. I stepped into the shower and ran the warm water on my hand first then allowed the shower head to pour water on my face. I started singing the same song by Tasha Cobbs that had played in the car when I was with my dad the previous day. I hummed to myself before singing aloud, washing each part of my body.

I stepped out of the shower and wrapped the towel around me before heading out of the room. "That's a beautiful song, sweetie. I didn't know you could sing like that," I heard my dad whisper.

"Daddy?" I said, making sure the towel was wrapped around me tightly. You up already?"

He chuckled. "That's the same thing I thought about you. I said to myself, `Taneshia usually sleeps until ten a.m.'" I nodded in agreement and walked toward him to receive his hug.

"Yeah, I got up early to take a shower. I fell asleep last night. I was gonna lay back down."

"Okay, go ahead and do that. Maybe you and I can go walking in a few hours and then get breakfast started. What you think, eight a.m.?"

"Yeah, eight a.m. is good. I'll set my alarm."

"Okay, see you then, baby."

"Okay," I said, walking to my room."

Wow, Dad knows you better than you think. Are you sure you need to have this conversation with him? Maybe the same epiphany you had about your grandmother is true for your dad too. He is loving you the best he can. Maybe everyone is loving you the best they can, Taneshia. Maybe these conversations you want to have with your dad, grandmother, and others all don't need to be as formal as you're planning. Bringing up old situations doesn't help anything, Taneshia. Maybe you should just experience being in a relationship with them as is and let them love you the way they want to love you.

I didn't have time to go back and forth with my thoughts. I wanted to take a nap before we went walking. I grabbed some leggings and a t-shirt and put them on before lying back down, trying to decide what to do. This trip was showing me that my family did put forth energy to get to know me and love me. Maybe the distance had prevented us from having a relationship. Plus, they didn't know I even desired a relationship. That part was my job. I had to make it known that I desired and needed a relationship where I felt loved and seen. This walk would be a good opportunity to tell my dad how I felt. We'd be alone, and I could bring it up gently.

I heard a knock booming at the door. Was it already eight a.m.? "Hey," I said, half asleep.

My dad opened the door, his shoulders jumping from laughter at the idea of me getting out of bed to walk with him. "You wanna sleep some more?" he asked.

"No, no, I'm ready, Dad," I said, getting out of bed. Are we gonna walk slow or fast? I've got some tennis shoes but don't feel like putting them on."

"Nah, your old dad can't walk as fast as I used to with these knees. Wear your flats," he said, pointing to my shoes. "You wanna drive to the park or walk there; it's about two blocks down."

"Dad ..." I chuckled, shaking my head. "Let's walk to the park ... Duh!" We both burst into laughter, thinking about how silly it would be to drive to the park.

"You can tell your old dad don't do too much walking anymore."

"Whatever you wanna do, let's do it. I want to be mindful of your knees."

"No, no, you're right; let's walk."

We started out of the house and walked on the sidewalk in the neighborhood. "I brought you some water," he said, passing me a bottle.

I paused for a moment in thought. *Dad is so thoughtful. I was just thinking about water. Wow, he really does think of me and my needs.* "Thanks, Dad," I said, surprised.

"You're welcome, daughter," he said, wrapping his arm around mine. "It's gonna be a hot one today; you can already feel it," he said, fanning his face with his hands.

"I know. I'm glad we're out here early."

"Well, daughter, let me tell you the agenda for the next few days. Today, we are gonna go to Grandma's birthday dinner. Tomorrow, I thought you and I could take a boat ride in Yober City. We'll have a nice dinner and relax. What do you think?"

"I think that's great!" I said. My dad was good at making dinner plans and asking me what I wanted to do, then finding the perfect places to take me. Whenever I told him what I wanted to do when we were on the phone, he'd have it in place by the time I got there.

"Today is gonna be kinda chill, daughter."

"That's okay with me. I have to start looking for another job."

"Oh no! what happened?"

"I'm just tired, Dad. I really don't think I'm cut out for social work anymore. I never wanna go to work, and when I am there, I'm just drained. And recently, I was told I couldn't get the rest of my hours for my license because my current position is not clinical enough. My coworker texted me while I was here, telling me about more work they have given us. It's just too much," I confessed, almost in tears.

My dad embraced me and held my hand. "Do what you have to do, baby. If you're not happy anymore, it's not worth it. You used to love helping people. What changed?"

"I still do. But I think I want to help people in a different way.

I really wanna write a book, but I don't know if anyone would buy it," I said with my head down in shame.

"Well, you'll never know if you don't write it. Your uncle Williams wrote a book. You should talk to him about it. What do you want to write about?"

"I don't know. My life, I guess. But I'm not sure where to start."

"Keep praying, baby. God will guide you."

Before we knew it, we were back at the house.

"Wow, I wish we could go walking together all the time. We already walked for two miles, Taneshia! Thank you, Jesus."

I looked at my dad with a grin. Things were starting to become clearer. My dad *did* love me, but the distance between us made it hard to spend time together. In turn, we didn't really know each other. I made up my mind; instead of talking to him about what he'd done or where he'd been when I was little, and all those other questions about the past that felt too awkward to bring up, I would focus on the future. I'd talk to him about ways to spend more time. Maybe we could do virtual calls, or I could come down to visit more often. Maybe I could even move closer.

We walked back into the house, smiling and laughing about old memories, and I felt good.

As we entered the house, we saw my stepmom sitting on the couch, watching the news. "Oh, you two got an early start today, huh?" she said, looking at me with open arms.

I gave her a kiss on the cheek. "Hey, Vanessa," I said.

"Hi, sweetie," she said with a smile.

"Vanessa, guess what Taneshia wants for breakfast," my dad said.

"What?"

"Cheese toast, turkey bacon, and eggs!" he said, slapping his hands together with a chuckle.

"Yeah, you're your daddy's daughter. I don't see how y'all eat cheese on toast." We all shared a giggle.

I started toward the kitchen to help Dad.

"Where you going?" Vanessa asked.

"To the kitchen," I said, pointing that way.

"No, no, no child! You're on vacation. Jay, you can cook that breakfast by yourself. Taneshia is on vacation. Don't nobody wanna cook on vacation."

I looked at my dad, confused about what to do. "Sit down, Taneshia. I got it," my dad said, shaking his head.

"Are you sure, Dad?"

He gave me a thumbs up to confirm.

"So, what's new? We haven't talked," Vanessa said.

"Not too much. I hate my job, still not dating, and I'm thinking about writing a book."

Vanessa's face dropped. "Oh, I see we got a lot to catch up on. You hate your job? You love helping people."

"That's what I said ..." my dad shouted, giving his two cents from the kitchen.

I put my head down, still ashamed that I felt this way about the career path I once loved. "I know. It just doesn't inspire me anymore. And my clients have so much past trauma that it really makes it hard to support them in getting the services they need. Many of my families have a history of being chronically homeless."

"Wow! I always told your dad you do some hard work. It doesn't surprise me that you're tired," she said, crossing her legs and glancing at the TV.

"Yeah," I said. I looked at the TV too. She was watching one of their favorite shows, *CSI Miami.* I like comedies, so stuff like that bored me to death.

I went into the guest room and grabbed my phone. I had three missed text messages from Ashton, and Joanne had called once and texted four times. I checked Joanne's message first: Hey, girl! Sorry again about last night. Give me a call. It's been so much going on with my boyfriend. I hope you're well.

The second message: Hey, girl. Haven't heard from you. Hope all is well. I hope you aren't mad at me about yesterday. I was only trying to help.

Then the third message: Wow! Well, I guess you're busy. TTYL!

I read the time of each message. They were all about thirty minutes apart. I was confused. This wasn't new for Joanne when she needed support, but I was disappointed that she was doing this now, when I needed her support the most. She knew I was with my dad, and she knew I was struggling. Did I not make that clear enough? I thought I had the day before. I had my own problems to deal with; I didn't have the capacity to support Joanne, and I thought I'd explained that in so many words.

I shook my head in disgust and then read Ashton's messages.

What the hell does this man want, I thought as I started reading the first one: Hey, baby. I hope all is well. I miss you. How is everything with your pops? I can't wait for you to come home. I really miss you. Love you.

Love … what the hell?! This man really thinks I'm slow as hell. Love me? All we do is go out to dinner, hang out, and text. No real intimacy. Just a few laughs, and then I'm taking the train or an Uber home—alone. Love how? What is going on? What am I doing?

I deleted Ashton's and Joanne's messages with no response. I was questioning everything about myself. This whole thing with

Ashton was too much. I was never supposed to have anything but a friendship with him. I'd met him in a bar one Friday night with friends. He asked me for my phone number, and he texted me the same night. His texts and calls were frequent, and it made me feel special and loved. Ashton would send me a text just to say he was thinking of me. No one had ever done that before. Guys in the past treated me like I got on their nerves. I would text them and couldn't get a response. Call, and no answer. Even when I gave all of myself to them, I still wouldn't get the love and affection I deserved. Love felt hopeless. But this experience with Ashton was different. He would send little gifts to my job all the time, take me on dinner dates, have long phone calls with me before bed, and do everything I could imagine I wanted from a man. I was so happy! And then he dropped the bomb that he didn't believe in monogamy and had multiple girlfriends. I was crushed. I thought I was that woman who would come into his life to show him how amazing he was and how I could make him better. I thought being open, understanding, and easy going would show him that there was a woman who could love him as he was and how he deserved, leaving him no reason to date other women.

As I was healing, I could see how Ashton preyed on me. When he'd met me three years ago at that bar, I was still dealing with severe depression. That night, I had pulled myself out of bed to go out with Joanne. There I was in all black, wearing a wig that was crooked on my head and glasses with a cracked frame, smiling with my friends. And there he was, caramel skin, bald head, standing six feet, with huge muscles and a gorgeous smile with dimples. When he first approached, I automatically assumed he was trying to talk to Joanne, so I looked away. But he tapped me on my shoulder and introduced himself. I smiled, and we talked for at least an hour. He even bought drinks for me and two of my friends. The bar was getting ready to close, so we exchanged phone numbers, and we'd been close ever since.

During the first year, we really were just friends. I heard from him every now and again, and I didn't mind because it was a full-time job dealing with my depression and trying to manage my life. Back then, a good day consisted of getting up, putting my wig on straight, and getting to work on time. On a great day, my clothes matched, and I was able to lay my baby hairs down. However, by year two, he started asking me to hang out more. I was nervous at first. He was so handsome, and I felt insecure with him. I wondered why he was with me instead of another woman who was more beautiful than me. But he kept asking me out, and we always had a great time, so I just assumed, after a while, that I was beautiful *to him*.

In the beginning, it was great. Looking back, I would even say I needed Ashton at that time. Being with him helped me break out of my shell. Between therapy and his consistent attention, I felt great. I felt needed and important. He always told me how gorgeous and smart I was and how he had never met a woman like me. I started buying new clothes, trying new hairstyles, and even makeup. We went shopping together and he bought me clothes, accessories, beautiful scarfs, and earrings.

He made me feel like I was his, and he was mine. But as time went on, I felt more like he was grooming me. He hinted at various sexual acts he wanted to try, and I'd just laugh it off. He'd send me inappropriate messages about sex videos he had made with other women. Most of the time, I didn't respond. Occasionally, I'd just send back a smiley face or two to avoid the awkwardness.

I didn't know what to say. Ashton knew I was a Christian and didn't believe in pre-marital sex.

Eventually, the kisses and hugs increased, and I enjoyed them. But then he started getting upset when I couldn't go out with him all the time. If I made other plans or just wanted to rest, Ashton would say he understood but wouldn't talk to me for a week after. I'd text him but get no response for a few days. I started feeling sad and unloved again. When he responded to me, I apologized constantly and promised him I would be available next time. He'd forgive me, and things would be great again. Most of the time, I didn't understand what I was asking forgiveness for; I just feared that if I didn't, he would stop talking to me, and I wouldn't have anyone to love me.

As long as I was doing what he wanted me to do, things were fine. But as soon as I set a boundary or questioned what we were doing, the emotional abuse and gaslighting would start. He said things like, "You have an attitude today. I don't need that energy," or "Wow, you woke up on the wrong side of the bed. Maybe I should call you in a few days and let you think about what you just said to me." Because I was, indeed, emotional, struggling with depression, and had low self-esteem, I felt guilty and believed I was ruining our relationship by questioning him or having an opinion.

This was the cycle of our relationship for the last two years. But my healing work was raising my self-awareness, and I could clearly see my actions in all my relationships for the first time in my life. I was convinced that Ashton had been manipulating me during our entire relationship. He was a narcissist.

In addition to dealing with Ashton's mess, I hated my job, but I had been doing social work my entire life, and I didn't know what other profession to try. The job I had was a city job with good benefits and pay. I had worked hard to get it, but now that I had it, I still wasn't satisfied. I was tired of complaining and crying about being unhappy, but I didn't know what else to do. I couldn't keep living this way, minimizing my own needs and feelings. I knew change had to happen; I just didn't know how to do it yet. I was hoping by seeing my dad and sharing my feelings with him, it would open a door for him to help me figure out how to get out of the chaos I called my life.

I looked at Vanessa and saw that she had fallen back asleep. She had her glasses on to read a book, but her eyes were closed. I smelled bacon and got excited. "Dad, is the food almost ready?" I said, eagerly walking to the kitchen.

"You know it is, baby! Grab those plates and set the table."

"Yeah!" I said, giving him a kiss on the cheek. "Daddy, I really gotta do something about my weight. I love to eat."

My dad laughed. "Well, Taneshia Johnson, that's something you got from your old daddy. When you figure out how to stop liking food, you let me know." We shared a hug and chuckled together.

"Not liking food … I don't even think that's in y'all family's vocabulary," my stepmom interjected, beaming in excitement about the food as she came to the table.

I set the table for us to eat. Normally, at home, my mother and I ate separately in our rooms or in the living room. I had seen people hold hands and pray before a meal on TV, but I rarely did it myself, until I came to visit my dad. I sat at the table and held my stepmom's hand.

My dad sat next to me and held both our hands and said a prayer. "Dear, Father, we thank you for this time we have with Taneshia Johnson. We love her very much, Lord, and we're thankful for the time we have. We pray that this food gives us the nourishment and health to continue to live in Your purpose. In Jesus' name we pray. Amen."

"Amen," my stepmom and I said in unison.

As we filled our plates with turkey bacon, eggs, and cheese toast, I was shocked. *Dad thanked God for me? Me? Why? Why would you thank God for someone who ruined your life, someone you didn't want to take care of? I guess he really does love me.*

I started eating my food, holding back tears. Little Taneshia was really having a hard time during this trip. I had never cried this much when visiting my dad since the first time I saw him at six years old.

We ate while watching *CSI Miami* on the television. Once everyone was done, I immediately started grabbing plates and cleaning the table. "I'll clean up, Dad; you already did the hard work of cooking."

"All right, all right … Hey, I won't argue with you, Taneshia." He sat on the couch, grabbed a newspaper, and began flipping through it. My stepmom made her way back to the couch as well, asking him not to change the channel. "Well, Taneshia. Me and Vanessa kinda low key at seventy-two, you know?"

I laughed. "Dad, I'm okay with the idea of chilling until dinner. I actually wanna look for jobs, scroll through the internet and all that jazz."

"All right, baby. Sounds good. Your old dad may take a nap here in a few hours."

"Me too!" We laughed.

"Oh yeah, 'cause you got up early. Vanessa, Taneshia was up at five a.m!"

"Doing what?!" she said, glancing back at me.

"I didn't take a shower last night when I got in. That is a pet peeve of mine, so I got up early to take one and go back to sleep."

"You better be careful, Taneshia. You're getting more and more like your daddy."

My dad repeatedly clapped his hands while quietly laughing. Anytime something was especially funny to him, he clapped while his shoulders jumped with a big, hearty chuckle.

"Really?" I said, surprised.

I noticed my dad always sought out things about me that reminded him of himself. I had been reading a lot of books about healing parent wounds and realized that when a man has a child, the relationship he has with the mother plays a big role in how he views that child as his own. Considering my dad was already married when I came about, I imagine that it tarnished his acceptance of me as his own from the beginning. I was pleased that he saw so much of himself in me. I was also pleased that I had done the research to learn this about him and didn't judge him for it. It was his God-given way of trying to connect to me, so he could claim me as his own.

As I wiped off the last dish and placed it back in the cabinet, my dad came and gave me a big hug. "I love you, Taneshia Johnson. I am so happy you're here, baby," he said while softly rubbing my back and rocking side to side.

"I love you too, Daddy." Tears had been welling in my eyes for a couple hours now, and I just decided to let them swell up and fall. As the tears came down my face, they fell on my dad's shoulder. My nose started to run, and I sniffled to hold it back. As I rubbed my nose, I hugged him a little tighter. My dad wasn't good at expressing his emotions, but I felt that he knew I needed that hug. He held me in the kitchen for a few minutes, and we rocked while embracing each other. It was the most beautiful moment I'd had with my dad in a long time. And even though we didn't say anything, I felt seen and loved by my dad in a way I had never felt before in my life.

Red Lipstick and Heals

Both my dad and my stepmom went to bed for a nap. It was only one p.m., and I was eager to start my job search. I didn't know where I was going to get a job that paid like my current one, but I didn't care. I had faith and trust in God. As I checked my email, I saw I had a message about a self-love summit hosted by one of my favorite authors. He was a relationship guru and, most importantly, a believer of God and His word. I'd seen him before in June 2018 but didn't know about going to see him again. This was a different event, with multiple speakers I had never heard of before. Not to mention, I had to consider a plane ticket fee, hotel fee, and the fee for the ticket to the event. "Hmm … I don't know," I said, clicking on the link in the email.

As I pulled it up, I saw three handsome men, who were, to my surprise, all speakers and authors. I wondered if there was any truth to what these relationship coaches were saying. Never had I even thought about coaching. Therapy was my thing. I felt like everyone needed it. What exactly would a coach do, anyway? I didn't need coaching; I needed healing. I scrolled through the email and checked the price for the event. "Ninety-seven dollars?! These people must be crazy; I ain't paying that! Who the hell are they to be asking for that much money?" Even though all kinds of doubt and negativity ran through my mind, I found my fingers still scrolling through the email. I read some of the highlighted areas.

> *How often do you show yourself love? Do you stay in toxic relationships with people who don't meet your needs? It's time for you to put an end to your pain. Everything can be changed by deciding to put yourself first.*

"Wow, I need this!" I said aloud. I continued to scroll and read more, then I saw an incoming text message.

I scrolled up to see who was texting me—Joanne: Hey, sis. Not sure what is happening, but please call me. I need you.

I read the text with curiosity and disgust. I was curious because I wondered what was happening, and I was disgusted because I was going through one of the hardest times of my life, and Joanne was, yet again, leaning on *me* to support *her.*

I decided to pick up the phone and call her.

"Taneshia, girl, where you been? I been texting and calling," Joanne said, sounding desperate.

I was quiet for a few seconds, trying to find the words to say without going off or using profanity. "Joanne, I guess I need to take a minute to really explain what I am going through and how I feel."

"Okay," she said.

"I love you. You are one of my best friends, but I am in Tampa with my father, going back and forth in my mind since my birthday about whether I should tell him how I feel, and you're calling *me* about *your* problems. I don't really have the capacity to support you right now. Silly me, because I was thinking you could actually support *me*." Tears began rolling down my face. I went to the bathroom to get some tissues.

As I looked frantically for the tissue, going back and forth from the restroom to the bedroom, I heard sobbing on the other end of the phone. "Taneshia, I have been there for you. I have been there to help you through this codependency journey! I honestly can't even believe you're saying this to me," she said, sniffling.

"I hear you, Joanne. And I also want you to hear that I appreciate that, but girl, I'm still going through it! I apologize that I was not clear. I thought constantly crying every time you called me would let you know the mindset I was in, but I can see that I have not been clear. I *cannot* support you right now. I know you have issues with your boyfriend and his cheating, etc., but I need time to figure out what I'm going to do in this next chapter of my life. I am thirty-five years old, sis. No babies. No man. All I have is my career, credit card debt, and the years I've lost living in codependency. I spend my days and nights praying to God and crying to my therapist, sis! It's been like this for five years. This is why I wanted you to come to Vegas with me for my birthday, so I could explain to you how I feel and what really is going on with me. But, as always, something else was more important to you."

"And why are you single? Whose fault is that, Taneshia?!" Joanne yelled. "What do you expect to happen? For a man to fall out of the sky?! You don't date; you've gained over fifteen pounds from eating your problems away; then you complain about it to me! You're doing everything other than what you're supposed to do. Now, you're in Florida with your dad, and you don't even appreciate having a relationship with him! You know how many black women wish they were in your situation? At least he eventually stepped up to the plate and tried! You were still little too, like six years old. Get out of here with that complaining shit! My dad is in prison for life! You're mad because I didn't celebrate your birthday with you … girl, bye! We're always going on vacations for your birthday, but I had stuff to do. I have a whole-ass man I'm trying to be here for, not to mention, help him with his two children. Everybody can't take trips all over the world when they feel like it like you! Everybody ain't making money with no kids to raise like you! You're complaining about your credit card debt, yet steadily running them up, traveling, shopping, and going to fancy restaurants, by yourself by the way, which makes no sense. You need to stop fearing rejection, get you a man, and stop expecting me and all our other friends to go places with you. Clearly, I have a lot going on. Plus, I'm taking care of my mom and my siblings, and you know that! I can't just jump on a plane 'cause it's your birthday! I got business to take care of, Taneshia!" She paused for only a second. "Hello … Hello?!" Joanne likely noticed that I hadn't attempted to speak or yell back at her for a few minutes. "Taneshia?"

"Yeah," I said calmly with tears in my eyes.

"Are you there?" she said, sounding confused.

"Yeah, I'm here. Joanne, I appreciate and love you so much. I think I will never really be able to express how thankful I am that God used you as a vessel five years ago to help me see the error of my ways. Remember when I saw you at the first codependency meeting I went to, and I left early?" I said, sniffling and giggling.

"Yeah, yeah, I do," she said with a chuckle. "And I told you I was there for you," she added, this time with more patience in her tone.

"Yeah. You and I went to meetings together and really supported each other. Yes, I was still eating, and you were still dating random guys, but we were doing the work, right?" I asked.

"Yeah, we were," she said.

"Well, I think this is a new level of the work … accepting when a friendship has transitioned and realizing that we are hurting each other more than helping. I don't want any toxic relationships in my life. I'm not saying we're no longer friends, but I am saying that, because I love you, I have to take a minute to get my needs together. I thought I could be in this place of healing and growing while supporting you, but I see now, not only have I not been doing it, but I can't even do what I thought I was doing. Am I making sense?" I asked.

"Wait … wait … what? Taneshia, what is happening right now?" Joanne said frantically.

"I'm saying I love you, Joanne. And because I love you, I've gotta take a break from supporting you. I think somewhere down the line, we forgot that we could also become codependent with each other. In this case, I feel like I am the codependent, and you are the dependent. I didn't think it was possible, but based on how we're talking to each other right now, I can see it clearly," I explained.

All I heard was Joanne sobbing on the other line.

"I know, I know, this is the part they don't prepare you for in the twelve-step group, right? The idea that you have created codependent/dependent relationships with people, even while trying to heal from the shit. It's wild, man," I said, sniffling and blowing my nose. "We've been through a lot. Me giving you money; you talking me off the ledge; me helping you babysit and giving you rides; hearing all the crazy stories about random guys; you listening to all my crazy stories … But we're not helping each other, sis. We're just sharing trauma stories, stirring the pot, but nothing in it is worth serving up. I've got work to do, sis. I don't know how I'mma have this conversation with my dad or heal parts of me I thought were healed, but I can see now that only God can help me. I apologize for putting so much on you and expecting you to be there all the time. I need to learn to go through things on my own, without always leaning on you or any other friend, or any other person in this world, really. I need to lean on God and myself."

Joanne cried while trying to speak, this time harder than before. "Taneshia, please … what are you saying?"

"I'm saying I think I need to step back and focus on myself. I want to be your friend, but I want to be a better me first." There was a long pause for a while; I heard Joanne blowing her nose and crying. A few moments later, I heard a stifling silence. I looked at the phone in my hand for a few minutes and cried, questioning whether I had made the right decision.

Taneshia, Lord Jesus! What have you done? This is your friend! Okay, yeah, maybe she did bring a lot of drama, never can keep any money, a job, or a man, but she's trying! She even told you about codependency, and now, when you start healing, you give her the boot? Wow!

I stood up and looked at myself in the mirror. My thoughts were taunting me.

You don't get it. What she did was verbal and emotional abuse! She's asking me to put my feelings and emotions on hold to help her deal with her boyfriend drama … And here I am, trying to figure out a way to have a serious conversation with my dad! Then she's telling me that her dad is in prison and other people have it bad … nah. That is psychological abuse. I don't deal with people who treat me like that, period! I don't care who it is. This is the new me. I love me enough to let people go! Period. I'm not taking this anymore. I told her we needed a break. I did not say we weren't friends anymore, and she hung up on me! It is what it is.

I sat on the bed, looking at my phone, hoping it rang. After five minutes, I concluded that Joanne wasn't going to call back. I set the alarm clock to wake me up at four p.m. so I could get up and get ready for dinner, then I lay on the bed, turned on my side and cried. I didn't know in what direction my life was going. When was the pain going to end? When was the work going to end? Was I ever going to be at a place of peace and happiness? I cried harder, thinking about how much time I had lost in codependency and, now, how much time it was taking to heal. I was sad about Joanne, but I knew I had to have that conversation with her. She was being verbally abusive to me. What was I supposed to do, allow her to continue? It was clear we had become dependent on each other, and I had to end it.

As I lay on the bed, I just cried. I lost track of time and eventually fell asleep and awoke to the sound of my alarm clock. "Lord, that was quick," I said, looking at my cell phone and turning off the alarm. No one had texted me, except Ashton. "Ugh, Jesus! Here this man is again. I can't," I said, slowly getting off the bed.

As I opened the door, I looked around for my dad. He was in the kitchen, pouring water and eating peanuts. "Hey, baby," he said, looking up at me in adoration. "Sorry, me and Vanessa fell asleep on you. Vanessa's still asleep." He laughed.

"That's okay, Dad," I said, chuckling. I took a nap too.

"Well, if you're still tired, we're not leaving until six-thirty for your grandma's birthday."

"Nah, I'm okay. I gotta keep looking for work. I am so tired, Dad," I said, sitting on the couch and throwing my head back.

"I know, baby. I can see it in your face. What else is going on?" he asked, sitting on the couch next to me.

"It's just … I'm tired of explaining myself to people and helping people all the time. I need to focus on myself, but it feels hard to do. Everyone always wants advice or help. I can't do this anymore. I just ended my friendship with Joanne for a while, until I can clear my head."

"Wow!" my dad said in disbelief. "I remember her. You talked about her all the time. What happened?" he asked, turning toward me.

"Dad, Joanne always has something going on. Quitting jobs left and right 'cause they don't make her happy; drama between her and her boyfriend; then dating men with kids, but complaining about having to take care of their kids. It's endless. And I just …" I paused to catch my breath and decide if I wanted to tell him more. "I just really have a lot going on inside me and want to be around people who can support that and help without making me feel guilty or ashamed."

"I see." There was a long pause. "Well, baby, our Heavenly Father knew this was gonna happen, and He has a plan. It's going to be all right," he said while picking up the remote and turning the channel to a football game.

See, this is the mess, right here, I be talking about. What the hell! I just poured myself out, told him what was going on, and didn't get anything in return except "God knows, blah blah." I know God knows, but what about you? Do your job as a father and console me about all the crap I just said. How about give me a hug and tell me you're proud of me for focusing on me. Or what about giving me some strategies for how I can deal with Joanne better? Anything besides "God knows."

Sitting on the couch, taking notes of all the thoughts going in and out of my head was overwhelming. It was almost five p.m., so I figured I might as well get a head start on getting ready. "Okay, thanks Dad," I said, giving him a tap on the shoulder and walking toward the bedroom. "I'm going to start getting ready, so I won't have to rush."

"Okay, baby."

I looked at myself in the mirror. My eyes were red, slightly bloodshot and filled with tears. "If I cry one more time, I'm gonna scream!" I said aloud to myself.

I sat on the bed, crying and glancing at my phone. There were messages from random friends, coworkers, and Ashton but none from Joanne. She and I would get into arguments like this all the time, and then one of us would call or text the other, realizing we were overreacting, and things would be good again. But in this case, this was it. I had lost one of my best friends.

I got up, went to the closet, and pulled out a yellow dress and a pair of kitten heels I had packed. I looked through my makeup bag and found some red lipstick. I decided to put it on, hoping that maybe it would make me feel better. I smeared it on my lips and looked at myself in the mirror. *Well, Taneshia, welcome to grown woman status. It doesn't feel good now, but you will see in due time.* I proceeded to style my hair and put on my accessories for the night. I had to bring my grown-woman self to this dinner because my inner child didn't know how to do anything but cry, and I was done with her.

We left for dinner, and as we rode along in the car, I thought about everything I was going through. I felt maybe it was time to look for another therapist. I had called Dr. Jones about a week ago and didn't get a message back. I started to wonder about her. Did she still want to help me? Did she have time? This was another relationship I was questioning. Not so much because of who she was, but because of me. I could see that I had a pattern of staying in situations way longer than I should out of fear of the unknown.

WHAT DOES HEALING LOOK LIKE?

Coping vs Healing

Coping	Healing
Leaving a toxic relationship, but treating new partners in the same manner you treated your ex	Leaving a toxic relationship, remaining single while you seek therapy, coaching, or both and learn new communication skills
Blocking and avoiding people when they make you angry or disappointed	Learning to name your feelings, share with others, and try your best to come to a solution that works well for both of you.
Drinking, eating, or smoking excessively to block out pain and bad feelings	Allowing all emotions to surface inside of you, and using self talk, journaling, praying etc to determine what is bothering you
Telling yourself things are okay when they are not	Accepting you are not happy and sitting down with yourself to create a self care plan.

I took my phone out and sent her an email.

Hey, Dr. Jones. I hope all is well. I am curious to know if you and I can meet when I return. So much has happened this year, and we are only two weeks in. LOL. Let me know your next availability. I fly back home in a couple of days.

Thanks, Taneshia Johnson.

I hit the send button. I looked up and saw we had made it to the restaurant.

"Okay, daughter, help Vanessa into the restaurant ..." His voice trailed off and I couldn't hear the rest of what he said. But I knew he wanted me to help Vanessa.

"Okay, no problem." I got out of the car and walked to the rear of the car. My dad popped the trunk, and I grabbed Vanessa's walker.

"Taneshia, let your dad do it. He knows how to do it right," Vanessa said as she watched me struggle to open her walker.

"Oh, okay. Well, I know I can figure it out for you," I said, opening one end and then the other. "Let's see ... Okay, okay, here we go," I said, smiling while locking the wheels in."

"Taneshia!"

I turned around to see what was going on. It was my dad, yelling my name. "Yes, Dad?" I said, confused.

"What are you doing?! I said go in and ask them to open the side door for Vanessa. It will be easier getting the walker through the side door than dealing with the crowd in the front."

"I'm just opening the walker for her before we go inside. I

didn't hear you mention anything about asking them to open the side door, but I can. I heard you pop the trunk; I was just trying to be helpful," I said with confusion and sadness in my tone.

"Taneshia, I said have them open the side door. Jesus Christ! Go, go now, and ask them to open the door; it's starting to rain!" My dad jumped in front of me and grabbed the walker so he could help my stepmom out of the car.

I went to the side door of the restaurant, flustered, my heart racing. My dad hadn't spoken to me in that tone in a while, and it was making me upset. The little Taneshia inside of me was on the verge of tears per usual, and the woman in me was mad as hell. Who the hell did he think he was talking to? I went up to the side door, but it was locked, so I started walking back to the car.

"Taneshia! Open that door! What are you doing? Open the door. Jesus!"

"Dad, the door is locked. I can't open it; I have to get the staff."

"Okay, get them! It's raining cats and dogs out here! Go! Go!" he yelled, this time with wild hand gestures.

I ran to the front and found a staff member. "Hi, sir. My stepmom is using a walker, and I was wondering if my father and I could come through the side door since the front is so crowded. My father is trying to get her seated so he can find a parking space."

"Yes, miss, of course. Let me get someone to open the door."

"Okay, thank you," I said. I could feel my hands shaking, and my face was warm and flushed. Even though I had tried my best to bring Grown Taneshia to this dinner, Little Taneshia was making an entrance. Seconds later, I could taste the salt in the tears that had dripped down the side of my face and landed between my lips. I wiped my face and headed to the door with the staff member.

My dad was eagerly waiting with Vanessa. The staff member helped Vanessa to the table while my dad watched. "Thank you, Taneshia, I—"

"Let me stop you right there, Dad. I didn't hear you when you asked me to have the staff open the side door. I was trying to be helpful. I had no idea it would start raining."

"Taneshia, I understand …"

"No, no, see you had your turn to talk; now it's mine. Dad, I am thirty-five, not five. I don't allow people to yell at me like that. I understand you're frustrated, but that was uncalled for." Tears started streaming down my face, but to my surprise, my voice did not shake. "I'm going to the restroom before dinner, but I would appreciate it if you *never* spoke to me like that again. And I mean *never!*" I said firmly while pointing at him. "I don't tolerate that from *anybody* anymore!"

I ran to the restroom, tears dropping from my face to my chin, landing on my chest. I opened the door and put my head down, trying to hide the fact that I was crying from other people. I pulled a towel from the automatic dispenser, ran warm water on it, and placed it on my face, allowing the tears to flow.

Even my dad is talking crazy now. People really feel like they can say whatever. Is this how people talk to me all the time and I'm just now seeing it? What is going on? As more thoughts entered my mind, it just made me cry more.

I looked up at myself in the mirror, sniffling and wiping my nose. I grabbed some bronze eye shadow from my purse and gently rubbed it on my eyelids with the applicator brush. I refreshed my red lipstick and stared at myself. After a deep breath, I managed a smile. I was happy that I'd stood up for myself. I walked out of the restroom and back to the table.

I saw that my aunt, grandmother, and cousin had made it. I didn't know what they were talking about before I got there, but I assumed it was me. Parts of me cared about my dad's feelings but other parts didn't. I was respectful when I'd corrected him, and he *was* out of line, so I had no choice. The days were gone when people could say whatever they wanted to me, and that included my parents. I was finally realizing what it meant to put me first and protect myself from pain and abuse.

At that moment, I envisioned a younger version of myself sitting at the table, looking at me. I looked back at her and smiled. *I got you, Taneshia … I got you.*

chapter

5

I'll Take Some Drama
with My Coffee

To my surprise, day five came faster than I'd realized. It was my last day to spend with my dad before I went back home, so I spent the morning packing for my flight.

After the incident at my grandma's dinner, everything felt awkward. The next day was silent. The dinner cruise my dad was so excited to tell me about during our walk had turned into a night of meaningless conversation and occasional giggles. We ate, sat out on the deck, and held hands, all in silence. I didn't know what to think. We talked a little about family members and the weather, but nothing deep. My dad didn't seem angry, but the fact that he wasn't saying anything scared me. I was glad I had set boundaries and figured he just wasn't ready to hear the truth about how he'd spoken to me, but I still wondered if I overacted.

I always felt happy and sad when it was time to leave my dad. I loved him, but the emotional turmoil was too much to bear at times. The beginning of Grandma's birthday dinner was rough and showed me I was more than ready to have the conversation with my dad, and, apparently, he wanted to talk with me too. He knocked on my door earlier that morning, asking me to go to breakfast and talk. He didn't say anything during our dinner cruise about our conflict, and my dad never wanted to "talk," so I knew he must have wanted to discuss what happened that night.

In some areas, I saw similarities between my dad and me. We both ignored difficult conversations, but in his case, I was expecting him to step up to the plate and set an example for me. Looking back, perhaps that wasn't fair. On many occasions, I'd forgotten he wasn't just my dad; he was also a person just like me, who had flaws, emotions, and feelings, and who struggled to figure out his next steps too. During this visit, I could really see my dad as more than just "my dad"; he was a human being, and he was doing the best he could. Parts of me thought going home the next day and not saying anything was best, but considering my blowout during the dinner, I could tell it was time to be honest and state my needs.

There was a knock at the door. "Hey, Taneshia Johnson. You ready to go?" I could hear the happiness in my dad's voice, and it confused me. He wasn't angry?

"Yeah, I'm ready, Dad," I said, opening the door.

"Oh, I like that color lipstick on you; it's the same from last night, right?"

"Yeah, yeah, it is," I said, slightly confused about what was happening. *He isn't going to jump right into the incident.* Was this going to be another dry conversation like the one during the dinner cruise? I just decided to go along with it. Maybe he would bring it up later.

"Let's roll, baby!" he said, throwing his arm over my shoulders. I was baffled. If this had been my mom, she would have gone off on me that night on my way to the restroom. I knew my dad had a different approach, but to keep silent during the car ride home from dinner and during the cruise, and to put his arm over my shoulder the next morning was a bit much. What the hell was going on?

We walked to the car, and my dad opened my car door before walking to the other side. He got into the car and started the engine. "Well, daughter, this is your last day with your old dad. I'm going to miss you. It's been real fun running my regular errands while you're here. I have to stop by my rental property really quickly to grab the rent check from my tenants. Then we're off to Waffle House," he said while rubbing my shoulder.

"Okay, Dad, we're not gonna talk about the incident at Grandma's dinner before I go? You didn't mention anything last night, either, while we were on the cruise. Remember … you yelled at me, then I corrected you and ran off crying? Remember? Aren't you mad? I hope I didn't embarrass you and Vanessa. No one said anything in the car."

"Well, we didn't say anything because Vanessa was asleep, and I was sleepy myself. I looked back at you, and you were knocked out. As soon as we got into the house, you said 'goodnight' and closed the door. I was waiting for you to mention it. I figured you would if you were still hurt."

I looked at him in disbelief. Not only was he not mad about what I'd said, but he was waiting on me? What?

I thought, *Oh, that's sweet* … but then … *So, if I hadn't said anything, this would be another "undiscussed" conversation that's just up in the air ...*

I had a history of emotional moments with my dad, and no one ever said anything afterwards, so we moved on as if things were normal, when they weren't. I was learning that a big part of healing was dissecting incidents that come up and asking myself what they meant for me. This situation confirmed that I needed to talk to him about our relationship today. I could no longer continue to dismiss my own feelings and needs. My dad *needed* to know how I felt. "Oh, okay," I said and looked out the window.

We were on interstate 75, coming up on the exit. My dad made the turn as I started gathering my thoughts for "the conversation."

He drove up to the property and parked in front. "Okay, Taneshia Johnson, here we are. You want to come in and say hi to my friends? They haven't seen you in a while."

I was bewildered. My dad always did this, wanting to show me off now, at the age of thirty-five, even though he didn't want me when I was a child. Joanne was right; this was long overdue, and maybe I did have to just get over it ... but I couldn't. I deserved to have an answer. "Okay," I said, getting out of the car and ignoring my thoughts.

As we began walking toward the house, I saw one of my dad's old friends, Michael. They had been close since he lived in Alabama. "Hey, Taneshia. Lord, have mercy, look at you! Jay, she looks just like you," he said, extending his arms for a hug.

I opened my arms as well and embraced him.

"Thank you. Thank you." My dad held onto my shoulder. "Yep, yep, this is the princess, here. We're going to her favorite spot for breakfast. Guess where it is?"

Michael looked at me then looked at my dad. "Y'all and that damn Waffle House!"

My dad released a hearty laugh, clapping his hands. "You know it, Mike!" he said, giving me a hug.

I laughed too, amazed that my dad took pride in these kinds of things.

"It's good to see you, Taneshia. Your dad says you have your master's now in social work, and you're going for your license in therapy," Michael said.

"Yeah, yeah …" I didn't know my dad told people about my education and career.

"Oh, yeah; he is really proud of you."

I looked at him in amazement. I didn't know this. Often, our conversations were so short that I didn't think he paid attention to what I was saying. Most of the time, when I called my dad or he called me, he asked how I was doing, if I was on my way home, and if I was safe. Then he'd say "I love you" and hang up. To hear that he told people about me and my accomplishments shocked me.

"Um, Michael, I think I'm just gonna sit in the car. My dad said he would be quick. He knows I'm hungry," I said, trying to give the best laugh I could muster.

"You are your daddy's daughter, Taneshia. Okay, sweetheart, so good to see you. Take care, okay, and keep that beautiful smile."

"Okay," I said, slapping on my big smile. I often wondered if people could see my sadness through my smile, or was it so big and bright that it tricked them into believing I was happy?

I opened the car door and sat sideways on the seat. As I stared at the grass, I reflected on my relationship with my dad, but then I heard my phone ring. It was Dr. Jones.

I answered. "Hi, Dr. Jones. It's good to hear from you," I said, so happy she called me when she did.

"Hi, Taneshia. I was calling to let you know I don't have any availability for the next couple of weeks. I wanted to try and fit you in for February if possible.

"Oh, okay …" *Fit me in? What the hell? I've been calling her for two weeks, and she knows the severity of my situation, right? Why is she putting me on the back burner?*

"I wish we didn't have so many gaps between sessions. I haven't seen you for about two months," she said matter-of-factly. There was a long pause. Long pauses, for me, meant I was trying my best not to react but respond. "Taneshia? Are you there?" she said.

"Yep, I'm here. I really wanted to talk to you. I'm visiting my dad, and I think I might have the conversation with him this trip," I said, trying to help her see that I really needed this appointment with her.

"That's great, Taneshia! I really can't discuss the matter over the phone, but let's try and set up an appointment," she said.

"Oh, okay, yeah … Let me check my calendar, and I'll email you."

"Sounds good, okay.."

"Okay, thank you." I hit the end button. "I can't keep doing this," I said to myself. I needed regular therapy. How was I supposed to get to the next level of healing with this every-other-month plan I was on with Dr. Jones? Yeah, I had gaps, but when I had money, I booked a session. I wasn't sure who had $130 every week, but I knew I didn't.

My dad walked out of the house. He started the car, and we were on our way. As we hit the road, switching lane after lane,

I contemplated how to bring this conversation up. With no help from Dr. Jones and my dad acting like nothing was wrong, I felt lost. I decided that after we ate, I would just jump right in and tell him about the relationship I would like to have with him.

"Here we are, daughter!" he said while pulling up to the Waffle House parking lot.

I hopped out of the car, eager to go into the restaurant. My dad was behind me, smiling. I looked back, smiling too. "What?" I asked.

"Nothing; it's funny to see you eager to eat because I am too." We both laughed.

Dad opened the door for me, and I looked around for a booth. I found one by the window, and we sat, picking up the menus, excited to eat.

The waitress came to the table, and I gestured to my dad what I wanted to eat. He ordered for us, and then asked me if I wanted some coffee. I nodded in agreement. I loved when my dad ordered for me; it made me feel seen by him and taken care of. We both sat there, looking into each other's eyes. I had been there for four days already, and I was tired of my own anxiety. Even though I wanted to wait until after we ate to share my feelings, this felt like the right time.

"Dad, I have been really wanting to have a conversation with you."

"Okay, good. Let's chat," my dad said, folding his hands on the table and glancing to the side. For the first time, I could see my dad's anxiety. His hands were shaky, and he kept clearing his throat. I felt like he didn't want to do this, but this was about me, not him.

The waitress came back and placed the coffee on the table.

"Thank you, ma'am," he said, smiling at the waitress and picking up his coffee.

I glanced at mine and back at him. My legs were shaking underneath the table, and I felt my voice shivering every time I opened my mouth. I placed my hands on my knees to help calm the anxiety. "Dad, what happened when I was born? Where were you? I know I saw you every summer since I was six years old, but so much happened while we were living apart. Didn't you want to be close to me? Why didn't you move to California when I was born?"

I finally said it! I was so proud of myself but nervous about his response at the same time.

My dad cleared his throat again. "Taneshia, you know, when you were born, I had a family already. I couldn't just up and leave. I had a wife, two children … my life was going well. And then, next thing I know, your mother was pregnant," he said, picking up his coffee again.

I took a sip of mine. I felt my face getting warm, except this time, there were no tears; it was just anger. "And then, I came … Sounds like I ruined your life. I'm still your daughter; didn't you love me?"

"How can you love someone you don't know? Back then, I didn't really know who you were. I just knew my life had changed. You were here, and I had to deal with it."

My eyes grew big with shock. "You had to *deal* with it?" I aimlessly picked up my coffee and took a big gulp to avoid saying anything disrespectful back.

"Taneshia, this is why there's no need to talk about these things, because you will never understand. You were just a child."

"I see, well, I'm not a child now, so run that last statement back to me," I said, now feeling insulted in addition to hurt. "Because, see, *your* life wasn't the only life impacted by *your* actions. Do you even know how many things I've had to endure in life without male protection? Getting off work late; being scared constantly; having to make life decisions for myself at the young age of nine or ten. I didn't even get a real chance to just live life without feeling anxious or wondering if I was doing things right. It was horrible and traumatizing. But nah, you don't seem to really care about that. Now, I understand why; you kept looking at what *you* didn't have."

"I understand, Taneshia, and I am sorry all this happened to you. I told your mother that life would be hard, trying to raise you herself."

"What? So, what was she supposed to do, have an abortion so your life could be better?" Every word my dad said aggravated me to my core. I couldn't believe he was actually sitting there, saying these words to me. I appreciated his transparency and vulnerability; however, his choice of words was disappointing.

"That's not what I said," he added, raising his voice.

"But that's what you meant!" I yelled, not backing down from my father's anger like I had when I was younger. If he wanted to go, we could go. I wasn't a child. I could easily change my flight and go home that night. It was nothing to me.

The waitress placed our plates in front of us. My dad looked at me then at her. "Thank you." He looked frustrated, and I felt like I had been beating him up for the last ten minutes. "Can we pray over our food and then continue this conversation, baby?" he said with a sigh.

"Sure."

My dad prayed over our food, then I cut into my waffle quickly to avoid saying anything else to him. I was in disbelief about the hurtful things he'd said to me. *"How could you love someone you don't know?"* Did he really feel like he didn't know me? Here I was, mentally beating myself up for four days, just for someone who wasn't even sure they loved me. I was learning that a life of codependency conditions us to believe we have to work to be loved. We have to go above and beyond, regardless of the amount of love the other people involved are giving. Was this another example of me going above and beyond for a relationship that obviously wasn't going to grow? Maybe my father would never really love me. Maybe our relationship would always feel like an obligation to him. I needed and deserved unconditional love, support, and respect from everyone, including my father. And if he couldn't give me that, maybe this should be the last time he saw or spoke to me, and he could finally live a life free from me, comfortable in his world of being a father to only one child and releasing himself from me—the burden. The "oops baby." The one who had ruined his life.

I ate my waffle while looking out the window. My dad also ate quietly, looking down at his plate. I was trying my best to enjoy my waffle and forgot about the conversation that just took place. I don't know if he glanced up at me or not because I spent the rest of the time looking down at my food or out the window.

We drove back to his house in silence. I occasionally looked at him. Most of the time, his eyes were glued to the road or he was looking to the side. I assumed he was either upset or at a loss for words. I pondered on the concept that I was not desired by my father and concluded that was why I'd always gotten the short end of the stick with him. I was always left out of family gatherings, and, for the most part, I often didn't feel valued or important.

Why was I here? Why did God put me here to ruin my parents' lives? Why didn't He give me to people who really wanted me? Why was my portal into this world through these two human beings who had complex lives that I seemingly only made worse? I needed to find a way to make things clear for myself, so I could feel loved, regardless of how I thought my father or mother felt about me. But how? I still didn't know. And I was growing angry with myself, God, and my existence.

As my dad pulled into the garage of the house, I immediately grabbed my purse and unlocked my door. When he turned off the ignition, I quickly got out of the car. I wanted to get in the house, be as cordial as I could to Vanessa, and go to the guest room for the rest of the day. I walked in the house, greeted Vanessa, and gave her a hug. I mentioned to her that I was tired, and wanted to take a nap. Vanessa began to go on and on about taking me to her sister's new house and possibly shopping and dinner my last night with them. I shared with her It was important to me to do laundry, continue to look for a new job, and just watch tv and go to bed early. Vanessa shook her head in agreement with me and we decided to say our goodbyes in case I was asleep when she returned for the day. Vanessa seemed confused. I could see in her eyes she thought we were going to spend the last day laughing and sharing good times. I told her what a wonderful time I'd had with her while sitting on the couch holding her hand.

My dad made it into the house and sat on the couch next to me. I glanced at my dad and placed my hand on his shoulder. "See you in the morning, Dad. I am likely going to do laundry, continue packing and looking for a new job. I just want to enjoy the rest of the day and go back to bed"

"Oh, well okay, Vanessa had some plans for you and her, but

I guess things have changed." My dad said, looking at Vanessa in confusion. " Yes, me and Taneshia talked and she just wants to stay in and get ready for that early flight she has. I can understand that." Vanessa said matter of factly.

"I see, well. okay. I'm going to watch television and take a nap myself, maybe when we both wake up we can make dinner together? What you think daughter?" My dad said with an eager grin on his face.

"Let's see" I said walking to the guest room.

I closed the door, sat on the edge of the bed, and cried, allowing myself to sob for as long as I needed without judgment. I curled myself into a ball while holding on to one of the pillows on the bed and looked at myself in the mirror.

Just like I thought would happen, my dad focused only on him and didn't even hear the pain I was expressing. I was sharing with him how I needed him, and there was no apology, only explanations for what was going on with him and why he couldn't be there for me. I didn't want to hear it. Part of me understood, but another part felt like he should have figured it out and sacrificed for me. Why didn't he move and try to work things out with my mom? I had hundreds questions going off like firecrackers in my mind, but deep down I knew that wouldn't have worked. My dad had hurt my mom too much. She even told me about the time he'd tried to call her and get her to move to Alabama when I was three, and she declined.

As my thoughts droned on and on, what I heard was that I wanted someone to love me. I wanted someone to see that I needed support and do whatever they had to do to give it to me, even if it meant sacrificing themselves. I was sacrificing myself to make everyone else happy. I had been living in a reality of never feeling loved. It was like both of my parents had made a mistake, and I was carrying all the weight. I was exhausted. Their "mistake" was now an independent thirty-five-year-old black woman who had a master's degree, had put herself through school, had a good job, and was considered successful. I wanted credit for that! I wanted their recognition that I had done damn good, considering the hand I was dealt. I was ready for them to spend time with me, help me, and love me. My mom was doing the best she could, but my dad didn't even seem to see what I needed from him.

That's it. You've got your answer. Neither one of them were even prepared for you, nor did they want you. Are you happy now? Can we move on now? 'Cause I can't do this anymore. It's up to me to take care of me, and that's it. I am all I have. And I've been doing a good job. Me and God ... we've been doing a damn good job. These people that you're begging to love you don't even know how. They've given you all they have. They both took the knowledge they had and loved you the best they could ... It's time to live!

I paused my thoughts and looked at my face. Even though I was talking to myself in my mind, I felt like I was talking to a part of myself that needed to hear it. And I was, indeed, talking to Little Taneshia, my inner child, who wanted and needed love so badly but couldn't see that I was exhausted from looking to others to do it. I could love me—and that would be enough.

I wiped my tears, blew my nose, and proceeded to gather my belongings, placing clothes I hadn't worn back into my suitcase and throwing dirty clothes in a pile to wash later that night. I heard my phone ringing and looked to see who it was. It was Joanne. I didn't know if I should answer it or not. I partially wanted to because she and I had unresolved issues, but I didn't have space in my heart to hear any of her shit. God knew I was going through my own shit. I chose not to pick up the phone.

I placed accessories I hadn't used inside of my bag, and my phone started vibrating with two text messages, one from Joanne and another from Ashton. I read Ashton's first, since I'd left him on read for most of my trip: Baby, I miss you; it's been about two weeks since you've been gone. How are things with your dad going? Hope you're having an amazing time. When do you come back home?

I responded: Good day, Ashton. I am well. Not sure when I'm coming back home. Hope you're well too. Peace and blessings.

He truly had some nerve. What did he care? He, like everybody else, was either using me or abusing me, pissing on my head, then telling me it was raining. I was done with everything and everybody! Work, friends, my family. I was just done with all of it. "What a waste of time," I said aloud while throwing my phone on the bed.

I packed up the perfumes and lotions I knew I wasn't going to use. I found my red lipstick on the dresser and saw some red heels that matched. There was something about lipstick that always made me feel bold and strong, like a woman who knew what she wanted. I needed that feeling now more than ever.

Regardless of what anyone else on this earth felt, God wanted me to be here. He had a plan for my life. What if sharing my story was part of my purpose? I would never know if I kept telling myself no one wanted to know about my story. I began thinking, again, about writing, even going to that self-love summit. But who would go with me? And it was in four weeks. I'd already taken so much time off work. I shook the thoughts from my head. I saw a black dress I brought with me to wear, and I decided to wear it to the airport. Who cared if I was only going home? I wanted to put it on to embrace the grown woman I was and leave the little girl part of me right here in Tampa. She could cry sad tears for the father she wished she had if she wanted too, but I was moving on.

As I continued gathering things, placing them inside my luggage, my reflections resumed. *Maybe I should go to the summit. I could definitely use the encouragement.* I grabbed my phone from my bed and clicked on the email. I scrolled down to the bottom, where I saw a purchase link. There were two options: regular admission and VIP. Considering I was going alone, I figured I should get the VIP option. I wanted to be able to see all the relationship coaches there and take pictures with them. Luckily, the event was at the Los Angeles Hilton hotel, so I didn't have to worry about where I was staying; I could just stay there. I smiled at the idea of me making my own decisions. I had so many mixed emotions about my life and who I was becoming. It felt like I didn't even know who I was anymore, but I was happy to be coming to a deeper level of understanding about myself.

The day felt so long, even though it had just started. I wanted to make sure I had used it properly. Looking for another job was crucial. I had been looking for a job for about five months now, all social work related. I was done with social work, but I felt so guilty saying that. I had been a social worker for seventeen years; it was my life. I just wanted to find a way to reclaim my energy and myself. I had been working for the city for about three years, and a salary of forty thousand dollars was no longer appealing to me or my bills. I was becoming concerned because everywhere I looked, even other county jobs, didn't pay what I was making or it was something I didn't have the skillset to do. I scrolled through Craigslist and Indeed.com, saddened by what I saw. I sighed, tossing my phone to the side and laying my head on the pillow, feeling defeated in so many areas of my life. I wished this was someone else's life I was living, not really mine. Warm tears fell from the sides of my eyes, and I angrily wiped them away. I was done crying but concluded that I needed to release these tears. I pulled the blanket over me and closed my eyes. I was so tired after a tumultuous morning and early afternoon. I knew my body needed rest for my flight the next day.

Morning time was here, and I got up a few hours earlier than needed so I could wash my clothes and get everything packed up. I put on the black dress I'd picked out with some heels. I wore a denim jacket with it and my bright red lipstick. I liked how I looked with contacts on instead of my glasses, so I decided to put those on as well. I set all my bags by the garage door and decided to make a bowl of cereal before I left.

"Taneshia, Lord have mercy, you up and ready, huh, baby? Vanessa and I were worried about you yesterday. We didn't even see you come out of that room to eat or go to the bathroom. I guess you were just tired, huh?" my dad said, watching me pour a bottle of water into a cup.

I looked at him for a while, noticing that this encounter was much different than the others we'd had over these past few days. No hug or embrace; he was on one side of the table, and I was on the other. It made me feel sad and unwanted, but it also made me feel more confident in my decision to end my relationship with my father after this visit. I had concluded that no longer having a relationship with him was best for me. The emotional turmoil

I'd gone through, trying to decipher if he loved me or not, what his actions meant, etc., was draining me. I had gone through it for thirty-five years, and it was time for it to end. This trip had shown me that I would never be understood by my father. He would always view things as if his life fell apart because of my birth, but he was responsible and took care of me. I could no longer endure the lies he was telling himself and refused to keep pretending like I was okay, when I wasn't. I was hurt; I was sad, and it was time to put all these feelings to an end, leaving them there in Tampa with him.

"Yeah, yeah … I was tired. I got up in the middle of the night and had some fruit and water just to take my insulin; then I went back to sleep," I said while continuing to eat my cereal.

"I see."

To avoid this moment feeling more awkward than it already did, I took a few more spoonfuls of cereal then washed my bowl in the sink. I grabbed my purse from the guest room and started heading toward the garage.

I rolled my suitcase out to the car. As my dad popped the trunk, he reached for my suitcase. "It's okay. I got it," I said. My suitcase was heavy as hell, but with both hands, I grabbed it and quickly dropped it into the trunk. My dad likely knew I was being passive aggressive. He just took a deep breath and walked toward the car.

We both got in and put on our seatbelts. As we drove toward the street, my dad glanced at me, which was something he typically did when I was leaving. He'd always have a heartfelt comment to make, and today was no different, as if he hadn't experienced all the madness I had during my stay. "Well, Taneshia, thank you for coming to see your old dad. It's been a pleasure to have you here, sweetheart."

I looked at him, dumbfounded about whether I should call him out on lying or just smile and agree. After all, just yesterday, he'd told me how perfect his life would've been if I wasn't born; now, twenty-four hours later, he was so happy I was there? It smelled like bullshit to me, but I ignored my original resolve to be silent the whole way to the airport and decided to play along. "Yeah, it definitely has been an experience I won't forget," I said, faking a grin. I turned back toward the window, and before I knew it, we were at the airport.

I gathered my purse and took my seatbelt off. When the car stopped, I immediately unlocked my door and started toward the trunk. My dad got out too, but there was no point. I was already at the trunk, waiting for him to open it so I could get my suitcase. He walked slowly back to the car and opened his arms. I wanted to look at him like he was crazy and ask for my bag, but I decided that was likely rude and not God-like, so I opened my arms and walked toward him. I felt tears swell up in my eyes, but I controlled them. I refused to cry another tear over him. I realized he must have opened the trunk from inside the car, and I just didn't see it. This time, he allowed me to take my bag out on my own. Shocked, I looked at him as he watched me take the suitcase out. *Okay, so he finally got the hint. Well good!* I thought.

I dragged my suitcase out of the trunk and onto the pavement. "Taneshia Johnson, I love you. Call me on the layover," he said.

"Yeah, okay. Bye, Dad," I said nonchalantly, already walking toward baggage check. I was so happy the nightmare was over. I had conquered. What I had been worried about since the year began was finally over. Talk about being a grown woman! I was so proud of myself. I strutted down to baggage check with my heels and red lipstick, feeling happy and accomplished. The year had started with me feeling alone, isolated, and lonely. But it took a major turn in a great direction—the emancipation of my inner child and brighter beginnings for me.

PART

2

Setting Boundaries and Learning to Accept Other People's Responses

WHY DO PEOPLE PLEASERS BECOME DEPRESSED WHILE HEALING?

Healing Cycle

As we heal from codependency, we become self aware of our own feelings and needs. We find we are angry because we can see clearly our needs have not been met in our relationships with those we love. We have not been taking care of ourselves and we become depressed about how to live our own life outside of supporting others.

6

Me, Myself, and My Depression

had been home for about a month and was back to my old routine: going to a job I hated, avoiding my father, and barely getting up each day. This was one of those days when I'd managed to beat my depression and the negative thoughts that told me to stay in bed. I was on my way to work. Depression had become like an old relative that came over to visit but didn't know when to go home. I had learned to embrace it. I still wasn't speaking to Joanne, and I was dodging Ashton like a plague, even if it meant blocking his phone number, and because Ashton had a bad habit of popping up at my job unannounced, I started leaving work early most days. I had to do what I needed to do to avoid dealing with his manipulation.

I started reading a lot of psychology books, and one spoke of narcissism. I wondered if he was a narcissist. He fit a lot of the criteria. One book titled, *The Gaslighting Recovery Workbook* by Amy Marlow-Macoy, mentioned the characteristics of a narcissist: "a person who only thinks of self, has no desire to support others, only seeks out relationships to get their own needs met, lacks empathy and understanding for others, lacks the ability to genuinely connect or love others, uses manipulation and confusion to keep others in their control." My mouth dropped. I was elated to see I wasn't delusional for thinking he was off, but I was also now curious to know how I'd gotten caught up in another "situationship" where I wasn't getting my needs met, and this time, I was caught up with a narcissist. My mind was blown.

I was feeling somewhat sad and confused. Thinking about Ashton, my dad, and Joanne constantly made me feel like I was failing in all my relationships. Even though I was happy to be on time for work, my mind wasn't focused on my job. I replayed moments with Ashton. There were times when I felt like he was slightly controlling and unclear. He would say things like, "We are special friends." I would think to myself, *What the hell is that?* Or "Don't tell people what we have because they won't understand." What was that? None of it made sense. I was happy I was questioning myself but also nervous about what this meant for me. I had become somewhat dependent on Ashton to support me emotionally. I had not dated anyone for about 5 years due to fear of the unknown and low self-esteem. I thought no one wanted me. So when Ashton came along, I was shocked. I was so caught up in the fact that someone I thought was attractive and a good man—great job, a house, two cars, financially well off—was into me that it felt surreal, almost like a dream I didn't want to end … until the emotional and psychological abuse came. It was becoming clearer that I was not happy with this "situationship" with Ashton, and it was time for me to do something about it. After all, he was dating multiple women; it wasn't fair to me. I had agreed to be with him because I thought I could change him. Now that I was realizing that I couldn't, it was time to exit stage left. My past pattern of staying with men until they cut me off had to end. I knew I wasn't happy anymore, and it was up to me to do something about it.

I hoped the self-love summit I was going to attend in Los Angeles would inspire me to tap into the woman I knew was inside, ready to live her own life. I had called Dr. Jones earlier that week and was ready to talk to her about everything that had been going on and confront her about why she hadn't been available. I was learning that speaking up for myself was crucial throughout this process, and I wanted to do more of it. I had plans to sit at work for about three hours, pretending to work, but really looking for other jobs, booking my flight and hotel for the conference, and then leaving for therapy.

As I placed my bag into a drawer in my desk, my phone rang; it was Ashton. I just looked at it for a second. *You know you really want to talk with him. Please help me understand what you're doing. This man gives you gifts, takes you to dinner, and gives emotional support. What more do you want? I mean, yeah, a relationship, but until that happens, he's good enough, right?* My thoughts harbored such low self-esteem, and I was tired of being tied to them—and Ashton. I decided to text back instead of answering the call. He had to learn boundaries that I had clearly not set with him before. I was at work. I had a job too. I couldn't just pick up whenever.

I texted him: Hey, boo. I'm busy at work today. How are you?

Ashton: Hey, baby. What are you doing after work? I made dinner plans for us.

Me: Oh, you did? I'm sorry, I can't make it; I have therapy.

Ashton: Can't you reschedule it? I haven't seen you in almost 3 weeks!

I looked at the cell phone screen and paused. Was this man serious? Who was he to ask me to change my appointments? Had I really been putting up with this stuff?

I texted back: I know it's been a while since we've seen each other. Today is not good. How about we plan to get together another day this week? Maybe before I head out this weekend.

Ashton: This weekend? Why? Where are you going?

I thought, *Negro ... why're you questioning me?*

He's questioning you 'cause you trippin! Just cancel therapy. You want to see him too, and tell him what happened with your dad.

"He doesn't need to know all my business all the time," I whispered to myself, quickly looking around to make sure my coworkers weren't staring at me while I had a whole conversation with myself.

Me: Yes, I'm headed to L.A this weekend, but I'm free tomorrow. You wanna go to dinner?

I wasn't about to go back and forth with Ashton. He had to learn that I shared what I wanted to share. My business was my business, period. I waited for about three minutes, but there was no response from Ashton. I started looking up flights for my trip. I found one with Southwest that left at one p.m. and arrived at LAX at two thirty. That was perfect because I would have time to take a shower and get ready for the conference. I booked the flight and a room for the night. It was going to be a quick turnaround trip, and I was excited for myself.

Before I knew it, almost two hours had gone by. I decided I might as well get a head start and leave early. I had started packing my bags when one of my coworkers came over and told me about a job opening as a behavioral health clinician. This was a position that would allow me to get my license hours and, most importantly, be happy doing social work again.

I glanced through my emails, searching for the job announcement. After about 100 emails, I finally found it. I completed the application and felt somewhat hopeless. Even though I met all the requirements, they desired someone who already had a license in clinical social work. I was still working toward getting my license.

I glanced at my phone; I had one missed call from my dad, one from Ashton, and forty-five minutes to get to therapy. "Shit!" I said as I jumped up from my seat. I gathered all my bags and headed toward the garage to get in my car.

While driving to therapy, I couldn't help but think about my trip to Florida. I hadn't cried since I'd been there. It helped me understand how a younger version of myself really needed to get those tears out. I had been doing research and studying the process of healing from codependency, and I was convinced that discussing childhood wounds was required to heal. I reflected on my therapy sessions with Dr. Jones and realized she never asked me many questions about my childhood in detail. She talked around topics related to my childhood often, and would eventually result in telling me I need to come weekly to really heal and feel better. She allowed me to go on and on about my feelings, and she seemed to focus on current behavior, which was great, but I was ready to go to another level. Anytime I questioned her, her response was that it was hard to go deeper because I was inconsistent with my sessions. I, indeed, was, but her fee was expensive, and I was doing the best I could to stay consistent. I wondered if Dr. Jones was a good fit for me. The fact that she wasn't available for a session when I needed her, combined with me realizing I wasn't going as deep as I would like during sessions had me feeling like this may be another relationship where I had to set a boundary. In this case, a boundary would look like advocating for myself and even possibly transitioning to a therapist I could see regularly. I was in process and thought overload and ready for it to be over.

I parked my car about two blocks from her office and started walking. To get to her office, I had to pass a cupcake shop that I went to regularly but was trying to avoid. I was always worried and anxious before and after talking to her. I never knew what would come out of our sessions, and this time, I was worried I may blow up at her out of anger because she wasn't there for me to talk to her before I spoke with my dad. I hoped a cupcake would calm me down.

I went inside and bought three cupcakes. After finishing the second one, I threw the third in a nearby garbage can. Food couldn't help me; only God and I could save me from the state of mind I was in. I had been doing so well. The trip with my dad allowed me to reflect. I saw how I interacted with Joanne, my dad, my grandmother, and Ashton. In all cases, I could do better at advocating for my needs. I was being mean to people, and then justifying it by saying I was maintaining boundaries. It just didn't feel like me. I didn't like this rough, one-word-answer approach to life I'd had lately. Yes, I was able to see my patterns, and yes, I was able to accept where I was on my healing journey, but I was struggling to figure out what my next steps were. I was committed to making my life better, but I lacked the understanding of what that looked like. I had made it from point A to point B, but the real question was how was I going to get to C, D, E, and F? I hoped to gain clarity in therapy.

I approached the building and punched in the security code to open the door. I knocked on Dr. Jones's door and sat down to await her response. Dr. Jones came out of her office and gestured for me to follow her. I got up, happy and eager to tell her everything that had been going on. I followed her with a smile, whispering "Hi, Dr. Jones. OMG, it's been like three months. You look great." I noticed she smiled but didn't say much back. Silence was a huge trigger for me. In the past, when my mother or previous boyfriends were quiet, it meant they were angry, and I would fear the consequences. Was Dr. Jones giving me the silent treatment? Was she not going to help me? Or worse, was she abandoning me? All those things had happened to me before by friends, boyfriends, and even family. God knows I went through it a lot with Ashton. I'd give, give, and give some more, and eventually, the person forgave me and came back to me. Her silence made me feel like maybe she, too, was angry and getting ready to tell me bad news.

I sat down in the recliner, pushing the button to extend the legs of the chair, and placed my purse on the floor next to me.

Dr. Jones sat in her chair and grabbed her notebook and pen while smiling at me. "Hello, Taneshia. It's been a while," she said, putting her glasses on and looking at me.

"Yes, yes, it has. Too long."

"Yes, definitely too long. Let's talk about that," she said. The piercing look she gave me seemed to be one of confusion.

"Okay," I said with a fake smile, wondering what we were getting into.

"Taneshia, you know it's so hard to really support you how

you need it when you're not coming in regularly." Dr. Jones had mentioned this to me many times before, but it seemed like she didn't understand my perspective. Did I want to see her every week? Absolutely! But could I afford it? Absolutely not. My insurance didn't cover therapy outside their network, and the referral I'd received from my job only paid for the first five sessions. I had been paying Dr. Jones out of pocket for the last five years. I saw her mouth moving, but I can't remember what she said because it took all the energy I had to calm down and self-regulate to avoid snapping on her and getting upset. I secretly wished I had eaten that third cupcake.

After about a minute, I opened my mouth, afraid of what was going to come out of it, but knowing I had to say something. "Um, well … it has been difficult for me. I try my best to come when I can, but the fee is a lot for me. And I know you've already given me a deduction. I am thankful for that, but it's still out of my range."

"I see. Well, let's work with the time we have," Dr. Jones said.

"Okay." I felt guilty and awkward. I wondered if she had any suggestions or recommendations because I was trying to figure out my next steps. I was tired of asking people for help. I thought everyone was supposed to do their fair share in relationships. All these books I'd read told me everyone should communicate and give equally in relationships; yet I wasn't experiencing that at all. My dad, my grandmother, my best friend, and now, my therapist seemed to just be leaving it up to me to figure everything out. I hated it! I felt cheated. This whole healing journey felt like a bad dream.

"Well, I saw my dad last month," I said with a shrug.

"How did that go?" Dr. Jones asked.

I noticed her face was blank with no emotion. I wondered

what that meant. I decided I wasn't there to analyze her but gain her insight on my own problems. "It went bad. I did mention to him how I felt, but I struggled to tell him until the end of my trip," I said.

"Mmm … Why do you think that is?" she said, looking at me over the top of her glasses.

I stared back at her, confused. Why was she asking me? I didn't know! That's why I paid her—to help me! *This is the problem, Taneshia, always looking to someone else to tell you what you know. I can't believe you're still coming here after five years. Really? Girl …* My intrusive thoughts had flared up and I was so sick of it. When I first came to Dr. Jones, it was almost as if three people were in the room instead of two. I would have long moments when I dialogue with myself in my mind while looking out the window, while Dr. Jones sat on the other side, calling my name. I glanced at Dr. Jones and saw her mouth moving, so I concluded that she must have been responding to me. "What … what did you say?" I said, squinting my eyes in confusion.

"I said why do you think that is about your dad? Taneshia, are you okay? I noticed last time we met you were kind of in a daze. Have your intrusive thoughts returned?" she said, this time, looking at me closely. I wondered what she was doing, trying to assess my body and eye movements through her tiny glasses? I felt myself growing irritated.

Here she was, analyzing what had already happened, and now trying to act like I was out of touch during session and talking more to my thoughts than her. Even though that part was slightly true, it was only true because I was tired of her and everyone else in my life trying to help me after everything was already done. I was tired of my dad praising me and telling people about all my accomplishments in life, when he should have been there to help me get into college, pay for school, learn to drive, and get my first job. I was tired of Joanne proclaiming what a wonderful friend she was, how she had helped me through chaotic times and telling everyone she was the reason I knew what codependency was. What about all the Fridays when I was at my church, studying on my own, leading groups? What about all the restless nights I'd had, crying and praying to God and reading books by Iyanla Vanzant and Melodie Beattie? Now, Dr. Jones was assessing me and asking me all these damn questions, when the damage was already done with my dad! It was over! I was done trying to maintain that relationship.

"I'm headed to a self-love summit next weekend, and I'm really excited about it. It's in L.A. Some of the most famous relationship coaches and poets will be there!" I said. Trying to change the topic to avoid showing my true feelings in session .

"Oh, really? Wow, that's good, Taneshia. What made you decide to go there?"

"I just want to experience something new. I want to find ways to focus on myself and really figure out what I need. I don't think I even know how to love myself, but I'm open to figuring it out." I folded my hands and placed them on my lap while looking out the window.

"Taneshia, I think this transition in you is really good. I'm happy you're taking more of an initiative to really identify things you want to work on. I am wondering how you want to spend the rest of our session today."

I was getting the feeling that she didn't want to talk to me today. The whole session felt rushed and off. I didn't know how to tell a therapist she wasn't being supportive, so I just sat there, glancing between her and the window for a few minutes until I finally said something. "Um, today, I just really wanted to tell you what happened with my dad and maybe even get some insight. I was able to ask him the questions we talked about, and his responses were tough."

"Okay, let's first go over the questions because I've forgotten. I'm sorry, Taneshia, but our sporadic sessions really make it difficult for us to connect. By the time you come to session, I feel your walls are already back up and your coping mechanisms are in place. It makes it hard to get to the rawness of you that allows you to be vulnerable." I could tell she was slightly frustrated.

I figured this was a good time to say something. "Dr. Jones, I know you have mentioned a few times about my sessions. I try my best to come every two weeks. I know we haven't seen each other in almost three months this time around, but that was also due to you not having an opening. I guess all I can say is that I do what I can based on the funds I have. So, if that isn't enough for me to get help, then I don't know where to go from here. I've been wondering if I should transition from therapy to coaching. I need more support for getting things done in my life these days, not just processing the past," I said confidently. I needed to make sure she knew I was aware of what she was saying and didn't agree with her. Seeing her every other week or once a month was not the issue.

"I see. Well, I'm glad we're talking about it. Let's talk about what happened with your dad," she said.

I was surprised to hear her change the topic, but I went with it because I was also getting antsy. "Okay, well, in a nutshell, after about four days of being with him, I finally asked him where he was when I was younger and why he didn't move to California when I was born so he could have a more serious role in my life."

"Oh wow, Taneshia, yes! How did he respond to you?"

"Well, he got a little offended in the beginning and then confessed that he didn't love me in the beginning because he didn't know me. Needless to say, I was done. I told him that I knew I was placed here for a reason, and I was going to fulfill my God-given purpose, whatever that is. I've been home for about a month now, and I haven't been talking to him. I'm still kind of in shock about everything," I said, this time, fidgeting with my hands and feet.

"Mmm … how do you think your dad feels about that?" Dr. Jones asked, taking notes in her notebook.

"Uh, I don't know, and I honestly don't care! Telling me that he had a family and how everything was perfect before I came was nothing a child should hear, whether I'm an adult now or not!" It was difficult for me to reframe my face. I rolled my eyes as I waited for her next statement, so I could clap back in defense.

"Okay, Taneshia, I can tell you're upset. We only have about ten minutes left, and I don't want to spend it talking about what happened if it's too triggering for you. Tell me more about your trip and why you decided to look into getting a relationship coach."

I felt myself getting a little calmer. I took a deep breath and began to speak. "Well, I decided to go because I want to hear what they have to say about self-love. I know I don't love myself as much as I should; however, I also know I love myself more than I used to when we first started five years ago." Dr. Jones smiled and nodded in agreement. "So, I figure why not go? I've been following them on social media for a long time, and I want to hear what they have to say in person."

"I see. Well, I know it's going to be a good experience for you. And, may I add one more thing?"

"Sure, of course, always. I just got a little upset, but I didn't mean to."

"That's okay. Never apologize for showing emotions here. It's safe. I know your intention is good. But I want to add that I hope you decide to call your dad. I would hate for something to happen, and you won't get a chance to connect with him." This thought was always the driving force that made me go see him, even when I was upset, emotionally exhausted, or just angry.

"Yeah, I hear you, Dr. Jones. I think I just want to focus on me right now. I'm tired of thinking about everyone else. I also think that's part of my codependency. Remember when you told me I was codependent a few years ago? I'm still in meetings, and I believe that doing for others is what got me to where I am. Now, it seems like you're asking me to continue that same pattern."

"No, Taneshia, I wasn't saying ..."

I started talking over Dr. Jones. It was the best I could do to avoid exploding on her and saying some things I didn't want to say. "At any rate, I will consider calling him."

"Okay," she said with a smile.

I could tell she was at capacity with this session, like I was. I glanced at the clock and saw that I had about five minutes left. I wanted to get some more clarity around this topic because I couldn't afford to see her weekly but deserved the insight. "Dr. Jones, are there any books about this I can read? I feel like I'm split. There are parts of me that really want to step into my position as a grown woman, then there are other parts of me that still desire my parents' love and support and an explanation of what happened."

"Well, it sounds like you got the explanation, Taneshia. The other part, I'm not sure. I have never read a book like that. Maybe you should write one." Dr. Jones got up from her chair. That was my cue that our session was over.

I got up too. "Okay, thanks," I said.

"You're welcome, Taneshia. Bye bye," she said and closed the door.

I walked out, feeling even more confused than I already was. What did this mean? So she actually wanted me to call him? Why? As I walked to my car, I glanced down at my ringing phone; it was Joanne. I eagerly picked up. I hated how things ended the last time we spoke. "Hey, girl. How are you?"

"Better, now that you picked up the phone. So what's up, Taneshia? Are we still friends?"

"Yes, of course, we are; I just needed some space. I think, somehow, we've developed a dependency on each other that just isn't healthy."

"What? No, I don't see that at all. Are you for real?" she said in disbelief.

"Yes, I'm for real. I just left therapy. I think this is gonna be my last time coming to Dr. Jones. I need to find a therapist who can see me consistently."

"Wow, you're really thinking about leaving her? She has helped you so much. Taneshia, this is kinda scary. What's going on with you? Cutting me off, cutting your dad off, and now the therapist? I'm not trying to throw shade, but I bet you didn't cut Ashton's narcissistic ass off."

I remained quiet. I wasn't sure if Joanne knew or not, but she was doing it again—projecting her feelings on me and pointing out the negative things in my life that I was already working on. Did she even know this was emotional abuse? I decided to ask her. "Joanne, when you say stuff like that, do you know it's considered emotional abuse and it seems like you just don't care? Have I always been this nonchalant and allowed you to say whatever to me?"

Joanne was quiet on the other end for a while. "What … I … I mean no. I'm just talking to you how I always talk to you, Taneshia."

"I know, and I don't like it. I never have, but I just never said anything."

"Mmm, I see. Well, what does this mean for me and you. I can't be direct with you anymore?"

"You can, but be direct in a way where you aren't bashing other decisions I've made in my life." There was a long pause. As I got closer to my car, I was tempted to go back to the cupcake store, but I knew another cupcake wouldn't help me. I had to experience all these things, including the drama with Joanne.

"Well, I honestly don't know what to say, Taneshia. I feel like I was the one who was there for you, telling you that you were codependent, and now you're pushing me away."

"I hear what you're saying, Joanne. It's not that I'm pushing you away; I just don't have time or energy to deal with the emotional abuse. The way you talked to me while I was in Florida was foul. And you knew I was at my dad's, but it seemed like you didn't care. You were focused on me giving you support, even though you knew I was going through it. You did know that, right? Or am I assuming?"

Joanne was quiet, and then I heard sobbing. "Yeah, I did, Taneshia, but I was just going through it and didn't have anyone. You have honestly always been the strong friend. I really don't know what to do when you start trippin'. I just be trying to say anything I can to get you back on your grind and out of your head."

"Even if that means being hurtful and mean. I see. Joanne, I made it to my car. Can I call you back tomorrow?"

"Yeah, that's fine." The phone went silent. I didn't know if that meant she was at capacity and couldn't support me or she was just done with the conversation. Either way, I understood and was ready to let the friendship drift if necessary because I didn't have any more energy for her or it.

I opened the door, placed my purse on the passenger side, and started the engine. As I drove toward my home, I was in a daze. I didn't bother to turn on the music because my thoughts were having a field day. *You really trippin'. You did this before. You start blocking everyone out, and why, because they said hurtful things? Your family has been talking to you crazy since you were born. Kids picked on you in school. And now because your friend made comments that are lowkey true, you snap on her? Really?*

I was taken from my thoughts by the ringing phone. It was my dad. At first, I just looked at it, but then I thought about what Dr. Jones said and picked it up. "Hey, Dad."

"Taneshia! Praise the Lord. I've been trying to get you for a few weeks. How are you?"

"We texted a few times last week, and I called you when I landed a few weeks ago."

"Yeah, yeah, I know. But it's not the same as hearing your voice."

"Yeah, well, I figured it didn't matter. What you said really stuck with me. 'How could you love someone you don't know?' So, I figured why call and worry you?"

"Well, that was a long time ago, Taneshia, and maybe I shouldn't have said anything, but I do love you now and think about you. But I understand it's gonna take time." As I listened to the words he said, tears came streaming down my face. I had tried not to cry these last few weeks, but it was no use in this case. I allowed the tears to fall from my cheeks onto my clothes.

"You know, Dad, I just want a real relationship with you. There are so many things I have to unlearn. I don't know what to look for in a man; I don't know my own worth. I feel like I'm just out here trying to figure out what to do with no direction and no help." I poured my heart out with each word I said and just allowed myself to be vulnerable. I didn't care anymore about what he said or the past; It was my obligation to myself to advocate for what I needed in the moment.

"Okay. I wanna help with that, baby. And you are worthy. You're worthy because you're my daughter and you're God's child."

I didn't say anything for a while because all I could think about was his words at Waffle House: "How *could I love someone I don't know?*" Now, here he was telling me I was worthy, and he loved me, blah blah blah … It didn't feel real. But when I opened my mouth, all I said was "Thank you, Dad. I appreciate that. I don't always feel it, though. I've been thinking about writing a list of things I would like to have in a partner, and maybe you can read it over for me."

"You know what, I'll do you one better. How about we look over it together via phone. Send me an email with what you need in a partner, and let's go over it next week." He did really sound sincere and genuine. I decided that maybe I could trust him to keep his word.

"Okay, let's do that."

"Okay. I love you, Taneshia Johnson."

I paused. The air in the background as I drove on the freeway was the only sound. After a while of thinking, I opened my mouth. "I love you too, Dad. Talk with you next week. I'll call you on Monday."

We both hung up. As I prepared to exit the freeway and make a right turn, I smiled. I was proud of myself for speaking up for what I needed. I was learning that, even though it was hard and felt gloomy, I really had changed and learned how to use my words to get what I needed, showing people how to treat me. I could tell this was the start of me building a healthier relationship with myself that was manifesting into my relationships with others.

I woke up the next day, still glowing because I had spoken to my dad. It felt so good to clear the air. I guess in Dr. Jones's own way, she helped me. However, it was clear to me that I needed something new. Codependency and people pleasing often stagnates us. We end up not leaving relationships because we don't know that we can. As children, when our parents/caregivers insulted us or made us feel bad, we couldn't pack up our toys and clothes and leave; we had to endure. We had to find ways to cope and survive. Those ways often looked like being passive aggressive, finding sneaky ways to get our needs met, avoiding interactions with people, etc. All those habits kept us safe, and for those who had psychotic parents, who threatened physical harm, it kept them *alive*. But when we start to heal and truly live freely, we must be direct, telling people how we feel and what we need, even when it's scary and we doubt the outcomes. In this case, I realized the harsh reality that I may have stayed too long with Dr. Jones out of fear of what a new therapist would be like. Parts of me knew she just didn't seem to understand me anymore, and I wasn't getting my needs met. But the old pattern we have as people pleasers and codependents is to stay in relationships and hope the person changes, just like we hoped our parents or caregivers would when we were little. My "Little Taneshia" was pissed that she had to step out of her comfort zone and make all these changes. Making changes reminded me of trying to jump through hoops, but here I was trying my best to leap anyway, regardless of my fear. I was a grown woman now and had to make grown-woman moves for myself.

I knew my medical insurance would help me with therapy, but five years ago, they only offered group therapy. I decided to call and find out about my options. I called my insurance company and let them know that I struggle with dysthymia (persistent depression disorder) and general anxiety and needed to talk to a therapist, preferably a black one. I shared that I was a recovering codependent, and sometimes the idea of setting boundaries, saying no, and dealing with my constant negative thoughts was just a lot for me. The representative informed me that, although she couldn't guarantee a black therapist, she could give me a list of providers that my insurance covered, and I could call and see if they had an opening. I was so excited to be able to choose my own therapist! I immediately looked through the list. I had about an hour before I had to report to my job, and I wanted to make sure I took time to do something I needed for myself. I found two therapists, but neither one had availability. They both asked if I wanted to be placed on their waitlist, and I declined.

I hated this process. I figured it would be like this. This was one of the reasons I hadn't looked for a new therapist. The process felt overwhelming. I just wanted someone to talk to; I didn't want to go through the leg work of finding someone.

I looked at the clock and saw that I was going to be late for work if I continued to look for therapists. I hopped up, got into the shower, and started getting ready for work. I fixed my hair in a ponytail and found a cute yellow dress in my closet with sandals to match. Even though things weren't going the best, I felt lighter, and my spirit felt at peace. Not being around Ashton or Joanne made me feel free. I could see how setting boundaries had changed my life. I felt good about communicating with my dad again, going to the self-love summit, and where I was in life in general.

My phone rang. I looked at it and saw a 4-1-5 number. "Who the hell is calling me from San Francisco?" I picked it up. "Hello?"

"Hi! How are you? This is Patrick from the public health agency. You applied for a position with us a couple of weeks ago as a behavioral health clinician. Do you remember?"

"Yes, yes, I do!" Oh, my goodness! I couldn't believe they were calling me. I was so excited!

"Great! I was wondering if you were available for an interview next week," he said.

"Yes, I am. I have lots of flexibility," I said, showing my interest.

He chuckled. "I can hear it in your voice. Okay, okay, awesome. How about next Thursday, March twelfth?"

"Yes, that's perfect; I'm free all day."

"Okay, how is one p.m.?"

"One p.m. works!"

"Great. Do you know how to get here? If you're driving, get

off on Third Street; if you're taking public transportation, the Number Nine bus may be the fastest."

"Yes, I'll be taking public transit." I knew the area was a little sketchy, but I rarely drove to the city and wanted to get a feel for the area in real time if I was considering working there.

"Okay, great. They run frequently, so it shouldn't disrupt anything for you too much. See you then, Taneshia."

"Okay, Patrick. I'm excited." I hung up and started dancing and singing in my mirror. "Yaaaaasss, sis! Who's gonna get that job? You! Who's the queen of social work? You! Who in this game is better than you? No-damn-body! Yaaaasss! God got you. You got you! It's about to be a celebration, yaaasss!" I broke out in old school dances, like the running man and the cabbage patch. God was surely smiling down on me! That sad girl that left Florida in January was a queen, celebrating her triumph in March. I felt like I was on top of the World. I grabbed my bags, put some red lipstick on, and proceeded out the door on my way to work. Life as I knew it was shifting, and I was loving it.

7

The Shift

It was the day of the interview, and I was nervous as hell. I decided to take the bus because that was how I regularly traveled to work, so I wanted to make sure I would still be able to do that if I took this job. As I sat on the bus, I started flipping through my resume and a few notes I had taken about the job description. As we got closer to the location, I began looking around at some of the housing developments in the neighborhood, which was considered low income, and one of the most neglected areas in San Francisco, but that didn't bother me. I was from a similar neighborhood called Fillmore. Going to the ghettos was not a new thing for me; however, I could already see how this area was way different from Fillmore.

The bus driver pulled up to the street Patrick had given me during our call. Litter covered the streets, and steel bars decorated light pink and yellow buildings that appeared to be worn down and rat infested. I got off the bus, looked down at my outfit and instantly felt like I was overdressed. I prayed no one got the idea to rob me, seeing that I had on high heels and would likely struggle to get away. *Taneshia, what the hell were you thinking when you were getting dressed this morning? It is what it is now!"* I read the address to myself while looking for it. I almost missed it because of the tiny writing on the building, which was tucked in the corner. I cleared my throat and walked toward the door.

I pulled the door open and proceeded inside. "Hey, hey, Taneshia!" I heard a voice say.

I looked to the left to see a tall light-skinned black man with a pot belly and bald head, smiling with his hand out. "Hey, yes, I'm Taneshia! Patrick?"

"Yes, ma'am. How are you? So happy you found the place easily," he said while walking toward a circular table where three other people were seated, all women—two African American, one Indian.

"Oops, I think I didn't bring enough copies of my resume," I said with an anxious smile. I didn't know if they were needed, but I had brought two copies that I immediately placed in the center of the table. Two of the women grabbed them while the other mulled over some questions in front of her, looking just as nervous as I was. I sat down, smiling with one hand on my knee, which was bouncing incessantly.

"No worries at all, Taneshia. I thought I mentioned I would have my team with me. My apologies for that. You're good. I remember your resume and have a copy here." He pointed down at a folder he had, which I was happy to see because I was getting the feeling that he may be unorganized. The current job I had was unorganized, and I didn't want to find myself in a similar situation.

"I know you've been with the City for some years as an employee, so I'm sure you know the drill. We have about four questions to ask you. After that, we will go over your responses and then contact you if we choose you for the position."

"Okay, yes, got it. I'm excited to be here with you all." I said, smiling. Sometimes I wondered if people could distinguish a sincere smile from an awkward one. I hoped that since they didn't know me, it looked genuine. The black woman who was sitting directly across from me had the first question. She seemed shocked to hear about all the experience I had. The entire team looked at me in amazement after hearing my answer to each question. Some of the questions felt redundant, but I answered the best I could anyway.

"A big part of the work we do in this community is help the residents here understand *they are* a community and that gun violence is not the way to rectify disagreements. We do home visits in this community as well as another low-income apartment complex about five miles down the road. We host events on the weekends to encourage families to come out."

"Weekends?" I said surprised. *Weekend? Hell nah! Girl, you know you cannot work on the weekend. Who's driving forty miles and sitting through traffic on a Saturday? Not you!* "Oh, wow! I think it's amazing that you guys support clients on the weekend. Does all the staff come down on the weekend, or do they take turns? How does that work?" I asked, hoping no one saw my eye slightly twitching from the thought of working on the weekends.

The Indian woman answered. "Well, what we do, Taneshia, is rotate; however, we do love when everyone can be here. It shows the residents that we care."

I care, and I also have my own life. My thoughts were judging her like crazy. I decided to just nod and say, "Right, I totally get it."

To my surprise, she continued with the questions. "So, tell me, Taneshia, I know you stated you have been in social services now for fifteen years; how many of those years have you done field and home visits?" she said, giving me the evil eye.

"Well, I have had seventeen years of experience in social work. From those seventeen, about fifteen of them I've spent working with low-income families, and for all seventeen years, I have done home visits," I said, making sure I spoke to everyone at the table, but my eyes landed directly on her face when I dropped those seventeen years at the end. *What you got to say now, sis? Yeah, go ahead and pick ya lip up off the table.*

"Oh wow, Taneshia! That's amazing," she said, looking at her colleagues around the table.

"I have a quick question, if that's okay. Does your department have company cars? I live about thirty miles out from the city. My current position offers employee cars to conduct client home visits."

"Yeah, yeah, so the City treats us like stepchildren. We don't get cars like your department does. We have to use our own." Patrick said.

I sat there smiling and nodding, answering all their questions, but the big question I was asking myself was did I want this job. They were smiling at me and each other. I could tell they were ready to give me the job on the spot, but did *I want it.* As recovering people pleasers, we must understand that things are different now. We are in charge. We no longer have to adhere to the rules of others. We live our own lives. And living my own life looked like me possibly turning down a job that could change my life.

The only reason I had applied for the job was to gain my license hours, but I was only doing that because everybody had told me, "Taneshia, you're so easy to talk to; you understand people; you should be a therapist. Don't settle for just being a social worker." I was listening to everyone else and allowing what they thought to dictate how I lived. That was an old behavioral pattern I carried as a people pleaser that I no longer wanted to uphold. I wasn't even sure if I wanted to gain my license hours, so why would I deal with an extra fifteen miles of traffic every day or unruly teenagers on the bus, throwing Cheetos and trash at my head? Or worse, possibly being shot and killed, trying to get home. It all felt like too much, and I doubted why I'd even decided to come to the interview.

I sat at the bus stop after the interview, sad, confused, and disappointed. I wanted to call someone, but Joanne was out. I decided to call my dad instead and give him a try. Maybe he could support me, especially now that we had talked.

I grabbed my phone from my purse and dialed his number. I cleared my throat, looking around to make sure the area was safe.

"Hello, hello, hello … Is this Taneshia Johnson?"

I laughed. "Yes, Dad. How are you?"

"I'm great now that I'm hearing from you. Hey, we're getting our regular weekly routine back. I love it. I love it, daughter."

He's happy to hear from me? I guess so. "Dad, I just had this interview, and it was horrible. Remember, I told you I was tired of my job?"

"Yeah, yeah, I do. I was shocked. You've been doing this for years, baby."

"I know, Dad, but I'm just burned out. I thought applying to other jobs would help. I got an interview, but this job isn't gonna work for me. It's too far, and it's in the projects. No shade to the projects at all; I grew up in them, but this one is known for gun violence during the day. And I have to visit two different projects on the bus."

"Bus? They don't have cars like the department you're in now."

"No, sir," I said, shaking my head.

"Lord Jesus. I know you're grown, Taneshia, but I don't like the idea of you being on the bus in a dangerous neighborhood, baby. Stray bullets don't have names on them."

"I agree with you. It's scary. I have to really think about it."

"Yeah, I know you could use the extra money, but I don't think it's worth it, honey."

"No, it's not, and it's not even much money; it's just really the opportunity to gain my license hours, which I'm not even sure I still want. It's just a messed up situation, Dad. I don't know what to do."

"Yeah, well, I know who does, daughter, our Heavenly Father. Let's take a moment to pray to Him about what you should do about this."

"Okay," I said while looking to the left and right. I glanced up at the bus stop sign, which had a meter indicating when the next bus was coming: eight minutes. It felt like I had been there for an hour already. I closed my eyes to pray.

I heard my dad clear his throat. "Heavenly Father, here we are again, trying to figure out what is best for Taneshia. She is worn out and drained from her current position. She has gone to this interview, Lord, and if it be Your will, this will be a step in the direction of happiness for Taneshia. Father, this is an unsafe and unknown place Taneshia will be traveling to every day. And even though we don't want to turn down an opportunity, we also want to make sure Taneshia is safe. We put it in Your hands, Father. In the name of Your Son, Jesus Christ, we both say ..."

"Amen," we said together.

"Alright, baby, it is done. Listen, did you start working on that list yet?"

I was ashamed that I hadn't made time yet to make it. "No, not yet, Dad, but I will a couple of days before I go to the self-love summit."

"Self-love summit? What is that? And where is it?"

I'd forgotten that in the midst of me being upset and confused about my dad I had failed to tell him I was going to Los Angeles the following week. "Yeah, it's a summit I found that talks about how to love yourself more. It's hosted by some relationship coaches I really like and admire. I figured I would go check it out and just get inspired, you know?"

"Yeah. So, you think you don't love yourself?"

"I know I don't. I mean, I can say I love myself, but if I did, why would I think all the horrible things I think about myself. I'm very self-critical, to the point that I put myself down before I can even get started."

"Really?"

I was kind of surprised and upset about my dad's lack of knowledge about my suffering. But then again, why would he know? Our conversations had been basic for most of my life, no real depth. I thought about my dad's life and his day-to-day conversations with people, and they were all basic. He didn't go into much detail with anyone, unless he needed to. I was coming to understand that this was just how my dad was; it didn't have anything to do with him not wanting a relationship with me. In his mind, he had one, and he had just learned differently a month ago, when I'd shared with him what I needed.

"Yeah, it's been a long journey to loving me, Dad, five years to be exact. After that Vegas guy, I was done. I didn't know how to bounce back; that's why I had to start going to a therapist. Oh, which is not working out anymore, by the way." I figured I'd toss that lug out there and see if he bit.

"What happened?"

Well, I'll be damned. He did bite! "She and I just aren't on the same page anymore. Plus, I can't come weekly or even biweekly. It's a strain financially on me. I know I need the help, and consistency would be a huge benefit to me, but a hundred and thirty dollars each session is tough for me."

"Yeah, honey. I think that would be tough for anyone except rich people."

"Right! I can't do it anymore. I contacted my health insurance and got a listing of other therapists they'll pay for. I called a couple of them, and nothing. So I'm hoping that the next few I call will have an opening, and I hope they're black."

I looked up at the meter and saw that the bus was coming. "Dad, I gotta go; the bus is coming, and I want to be alert while I'm on there."

"I understand, baby. Well, we prayed, so it's all gonna work out. Don't forget to make that list."

"Okay, I will. Love you."

There was a pause. My dad took a deep breath. "I love you too, Taneshia. I really do, more than you will ever know or understand."

I held the phone in awe for a moment, happy that my dad and I had this moment to have an open conversation, which made me feel supported and valued.

I hopped on the bus and headed home. The bus ride to the train felt so long. I was thinking about everything—my job, the interview, writing a book, and trying to figure out *why* I wanted to write a book. My thoughts spoke to me as if they were sitting right on the train next to me. *Taneshia, you have to stop these crazy thoughts. Ain't nobody buying no book from you. You're not a writer; you're a social worker.*

Do you really wanna take the train and a bus to get to work every day, not to mention work on the weekends? This is crazy. You get paid good money now. Find another way to get your license hours. This is ridiculous. Maybe ask Ashton what to do. He's always supportive.

Regardless of what my thoughts felt, I needed to do what was best for me. And what was best for me was making my own decisions.

After a long ride on the train, I made it to my car and drove home fast, happy the day was over. I hoped another department would call me for an interview soon. Would I really have to work in the ghetto to get ahead in my career? That's what it looked like. I would either work in the 'hood, scared and nervous all the time, or go back to making pennies an hour at a nonprofit agency. I couldn't go back to that. I took a deep breath and pulled out the list of referrals I'd gotten from my insurance company. I saw one doctor named Karen and decided to call her. As I dialed her number, I prayed she had space for me.

I continued to pray until she picked up the phone. "Hi, this is Karen."

"Hi, Karen. My name is Taneshia Johnson. I'm seeking a new therapist, and I'm curious to know if you have space. I struggle with codependency and low self-esteem. I got your phone number from a referral listing from my health insurance."

"Well, at this time, I'm nearly full, but I do have one opening every other Monday. Would that work for you?"

"Perfect! I will see you next Monday."

"Okay, thank you. See you then."

"Okay, great." I hung up the phone, feeling accomplished. I may have been unsure about my career path, but I had at least secured a consistent therapy slot for myself.

I took a nice, hot shower and put my favorite t-shirt on. Then I got on my knees to pray. "Dear God. Ugh … I don't even know where to start. I went to the interview, as You know, and I probably should take the job, but I just don't know, Lord. It doesn't feel right. And I feel like they're going to call me too. What should I do if they call, Lord? Give me a sign, Lord. Or do you want me to be my own sign? Is this a time for me to decide and just trust You? At any rate, I am excited about finding a new therapist. Lord, please let me connect with her. Let me be able to be vulnerable with her and get the help I need, Lord Jesus. And Father, please help me to break free from Ashton. I have been doing good not talking to him, but I really need to have a conversation with him about boundaries. I am scared. I feel like if I do, he may not talk to me anymore; then who will I have? But at the same time, I really don't want his support because I can see how toxic it is. Please help, God. I am unsure of what to do. I love you. Amen."

I lay in bed that night, happy and confused at the same time. I could remember being in bed, crying and looking up at the stars, desiring to be in Heaven with God but also afraid to die. I just felt stuck in a place where I was absorbed by other people's problems, with no way out. I cried just thinking about how things had changed. I finally felt like I was gaining control over my life. And it felt good.

8

God Got Jokes

had about two days before it was time to go to the self-love summit in Los Angeles. I was trying my best to do my job and found myself behind on notes for work. As I sat at my desk, trying to block off my calendar and prepare for my trip, I paused from my notes to make a list of qualities I would like in a partner. As I thought about the men that had been in my life, I tried to determine if any of them had qualities that I liked. Although Shawn and Ashton were easy to talk to in their own way, they were both selfish and untrustworthy. I decided to write my list based on the kind of man I had always dreamed about, instead of the ones I had experienced.

I sat at my desk for about five minutes just looking at the screen. I decided to close my eyes and pray, whispering in the hopes that no one could hear me. "Dear God. Please bring to mind the type of man You want me to have. In the name of Your Son, Jesus Christ, I pray and ask these things. Amen."

Before I knew it, my pen was moving. God was helping me discover what I needed, and I started writing it down:

1. a man who has a relationship with God and truly walks with Him.
2. a man who understands mental health issues and has empathy for me regarding my depression episodes and anxiety
3. a man who is financially stable and already taking care of all his finances on his own
4. someone who has traveled more than me and can take me places I've never been
5. someone I can pray with
6. a man who can exercise with me
7. someone who genuinely loves me for me
8. and has a love language of physical touch
9. Last but not least, he must be at least one inch taller than me.

I looked at my list in admiration. I was happy I had created a realistic list that I loved and fit my needs.

I was all smiles at my desk when I saw my phone ringing. It was Ashton. I reluctantly picked up. "Hey, Ashton. How are you?"

"Ashton? What happened to 'Teddy Bear'?" he said, referring to a nickname I'd given him when I thought he genuinely cared about me and was serious about building a relationship. I hadn't called him that in a few months now and wasn't going to start it back up.

"I'm doing well, thanks. I've got a lot of work to do today, though. How are you?" I said, ignoring his first comment.

"Oh, okay, so you're just gonna gloss over my feelings?"

"Ashton, I heard what you said. I haven't called you Teddy Bear in almost three months. I'm curious to know why you're asking me about it now."

"It's been a lot you haven't done in a few months. Every time I call you to check on you, you're either at home, running late for work or barely getting to your desk. Not to mention, we don't go out anymore or spend any kind of time together. This is how you treat people who have been there for you? Wow!"

"Ashton, I'm sorry you feel this way. I have been doing a lot of healing work, and I just needed time to myself. However, I am not going to apologize for taking care of myself. I have realized that our friendship has no boundaries. What you just did is called gaslighting, and I don't tolerate that kind of behavior from people anymore. We are going to have to find another way to communicate. This is not the time for this conversation; I'm at work, and I assume you are too. Why don't we get together next week and talk more?"

"Next week … You want *me* to wait until next week … I'm Ashton, baby. I get full VIP access twenty-four-seven to Taneshia."

I just listened to Ashton. I had never noticed how arrogate he was. The rose-colored glasses had been removed from my eyes. This was a sign that I was healed, and I could finally see what everyone else had already seen. I thought about what I had read in all those books, and it was clear now—Ashton was indeed a narcissist. He was all about self. Damn, how could I have done this to myself again? Even though Shawn wasn't a narcissist, I still missed the signs that he wasn't interested in a relationship with me. And now, here I was again, missing the signs. Ashton was in relationships with multiple women; I just so happened to be one who always got attention because I was always feeding some part of him, emotionally, mentally, hell, sometimes even physically. I had really put a lot of time into Ashton for the last fifteen months, and I hadn't realized it until that moment.

"Taneshia, T-Baby, can you hear me? This is me, baby," Ashton said, pleading for me to respond to him. "You're telling me I have to wait until next week? We need to talk tonight. What're you doing tonight?"

I had gotten caught up in my thoughts again. If he'd said anything prior to that, I missed it. I just wanted to make sure I made it clear to him that I had boundaries. I was leaving in two days, and I wasn't going to allow him to fog my mind before I went. "Ashton, I really love you, and I value our friendship a lot. Next week will be better for me. I have to get ready to go to Los Angeles."

"You're still going to Los Angeles, even though we talked about this? Sweetie, listen to me okay, baby? You just got back! Why are you leaving again? What about your job?"

Healing is a funny thing. When you start doing your own work, you can really see how crazy other people sound. I wondered if he was aware that the "job" he spoke of was really him, or was he oblivious to his own need to control. If he was a true narcissist then he knew what he was doing. And I believed he was.

"Ashton, I am aware. My time off request was approved by my supervisor. I'm trying to get things squared away here. That's why I keep telling you I really must go. We'll connect next week, okay?" I was hoping I was clear with him and he understood that he was no longer going to be able to manipulate me with his responses.

"Okay, talk to you later, I guess. Can I call you?"

Why does he want to call me? What the hell? This whole thing is crazy. I am not your girl, yet you act like I am. "You can if you want. I may be busy. I mean, it is a seminar—"

Suddenly, he aggressively cut me off. "Okay, okay, I'll just text, okay, baby? Bye." He hung up the phone, not even giving me a chance to say bye.

Wow, he is big mad! Maybe mad enough to stop talking to you. I laughed to myself. Sometimes I even had to laugh at my own goofy thoughts. I stayed at work for a few more hours to wrap up everything and then left. I couldn't wait to get on the plane on Saturday.

My flight landed in L.A. about three hours before the event. It was great timing. I was able to relax, grab a bite to eat, and change clothes before the event. I left the gate from the flight and started walking down the escalator. Since it was a turnaround trip, I'd only brought a carryon bag. I was in awe that I was actually in Los Angeles, going solo to a conference about self-love. I didn't know who this new person was, but I was in love with her.

I made my way down the escalator toward the exit and started looking for public transportation signs. The hotel stated that they had a bus that would take me from the airport to the hotel. I looked for it. As I approached the stop, I was nervous that I may be at the wrong one. I was known for getting on wrong buses and going in the opposite direction from where I wanted to go. I decided to ask a couple of women whom I saw sitting down. "Hi, how are you? Do you know if this is the location for the Hilton hotel bus?"

"Hi, I'm Tisha. Yes, it is. Are you going to the self-love summit?"

"Yes!" I said in excitement. "I am! I'm Taneshia. Are you going too?"

"Yep, girl! I've got to go. I told my sister she needs to come too." She pointed to the young lady next to her.

"Hey! I'm Karol. Nice to meet you. You by yourself?"

"Yeah, I am. I came all the way from Oakland to go to this event. I asked my friends, but no one wanted to go. I told myself I'm not gonna allow that to stop me."

"Girl, you better say that! And look what God did; we're from the Bay Area too!" All three of us laughed in excitement and relief that we weren't alone.

"Oh, wow!" *Thank you, Jesus. Thank you, Jesus.* I was so relieved. With everything going on in our world, I was nervous about traveling alone. It felt good to meet some people.

The bus pulled up and we hopped on. "So did you get the VIP package?" Tisha asked.

"You know I did, girl. I said. "Why not? I'm by myself anyway. Besides, after coming all this way, I wanna be able to hear and see." All three of us laughed.

"Right, girl, okay. I know that's right," Karol said.

As the bus driver made sharp turns, speeding his way down the street, we held on to the bars next to us and looked around. I always loved coming to Downtown Los Angeles. I loved seeing the tall buildings and flashing lights. It made me feel important. I didn't know what was more exciting, going to the summit or going to Roscoe's Chicken and Waffles afterwards. I decided to ask them if they were thinking about going to eat. "So, are you guys gonna try and grab some food before or after the event?"

"Nah, girl, we're going after. We only have about two hours before it starts, and I don't wanna be late," Tisha said. "Leave it up to Karol, and we would be going now!"

Karol laughed and tapped her on the shoulder. "Hey, don't be telling strangers I'm greedy," she said, smiling. She pointed at me. "Taneshia, yes, I love to eat. And yes, we are going after the event, so you might as well go with us, girl."

"Thank you," I said, holding back tears. I didn't want others to see me crying. Only God and I knew how much of an emotional struggle it was to get there. And now that I had made it, I felt like God was putting everything in place for me. I had even met some new friends.

We walked into the hotel entrance with our bags in hand and smiles on our faces. All three of us were so excited about the summit. I wasn't sure if they were excited about the content or how handsome the speakers were, but either way, I was just happy to have met them and not be alone at the event.

We went up to the counter and saw that about ten other people were standing in line, waiting to get checked in too. Karol whispered to me, "I bet they're all here for this summit."

"Oh, yeah, girl. You know they are," I said, agreeing with her.

When it was my time to approach the counter, I already had my credit card and license ready. I checked in, received my room key, and to my surprise, I saw Karol and Tisha waiting for me by the elevator. I smiled in awe. "Hey, y'all! Aw, thank you for waiting. I appreciate it."

"Oh, yeah, of course. We still have about two hours. We'll

meet you fifteen minutes before its time to go to the auditorium. I saw the signs. It's on the first floor to the right." Tisha said.

I listened in contentment. It felt so good for someone else to have everything together, so I could just follow suit without having to plan or figure things out on my own. "Okay, that sounds good," I said.

All three of us got on the elevator. I got off on the third floor, eagerly looking to see if I could catch any of the relationship coaches coming out of their rooms. I didn't see any, so I headed toward my room. I turned the key and took a deep breath. It felt so good to see a big, fluffy queen bed and soft pillows. I immediately dropped my bags, put my purse on the table, and sat on the bed.

I heard my phone vibrating in my purse. I grabbed it and saw that it was my mom. "Hey, Mookie. Did you make it safe? I didn't hear from you," my mom said.

"Yes, I did. I made it. I took the free shuttle to the hotel so I wouldn't have to get a car. I just made it to my room. I'm gonna take a shower and change clothes for the event."

"Okay, well, I'm sure whatever you need to hear, they will be talking about it. You're coming home tomorrow, right?"

"Yep. I'll be back tomorrow. My flight leaves at twelve p.m."

"Okay, see you tomorrow. Love you."

"Love you too, Mom."

As soon as I hung up the phone, it rang again; it was Joanne. I looked at it for a few rings before answering, wondering what she wanted. I hadn't mention to her that I was coming to this event because I didn't want to hear the negativity. I did consider her a friend, and I loved her, so I answered. "Hey, girl," I said, trying to sound enthusiastic.

"Hey, TJ! I miss you, girl. How you been?"

"I'm well, and you." I wanted to make sure I kept it brief with Joanne. I was still learning what boundaries would look like with her and didn't want to give too much information. If our friendship was based on me supporting her, I had to do that when I wanted to and when I was available to, no longer on her time.

"I'm okay. I called to support you. I thought about some of the things you said, and you're right. I'm in a dead-end relationship with a man who is not on my level. Fighting over what kind of bread to buy is crazy. I guess I'm getting bitter, and I've recently realized that my bitterness has turned into anger. I'm sorry if I took some of it out on you."

I could hear the sincerity in Joanne's voice. I felt the tears coming, but I refused to allow them to go past my eyes. I wiped them with my shirt and just held the phone in silence. "Wow, Joanne. I am so happy for you and the reflection work you've been doing. And I accept your apology. Thank you."

"Taneshia, I really don't want to lose you in my life. You're right; our relationship has become dependent. You always have encouraging words for me, and I guess I just didn't know how to be there for you. Hearing you go on and on about Ashton made me upset. You have so much going for yourself. Now, you're talking about writing a book … It's all amazing. Why waste time with somebody else's man? He's a man-slut in my opinion, going around having sex with any woman who has low self-esteem and feels down on herself. Think about where you were in life when he came in acting like a knight in shining armor. And now that you're setting boundaries, the real narcissist is coming out."

Damn, Joanne was right. I had put the pieces of the puzzle together for myself many times, but I was shocked that she could see it too. "Wow, girl! I realized that a couple months ago. Crazy story … So he actually had a fit about me coming to L.A. this weekend, but I didn't care. I went anyway. Who is he to tell me what to do, you know?" *Shit, you weren't supposed to tell her you were in L.A.*

"You're where, girl?" she said, sounding shocked and laughing at the same time.

"Uh, yeah, girl, I came to this self-love summit in Los Angeles. A lot of relationship gurus are here, talking about self-love and relationships, and I wanted to come and check it out."

"Check it out for what? Girl, I told you they be scamming! OMG, Taneshia!" As Joanne began yelling, I started drawing a blank. Here she was again, going on and on about a decision I'd made for my life. It bothered me because I was finally at a place of learning to trust myself and step out of my box, and I wanted people around me who could support that. I could tell Joanne was struggling with something in her life, and she was projecting on to me, but I also felt like it wasn't fair to me to have to listen to her berate me about decisions I'd made for myself. I decided to get out of my own head and stop her in her tracks. "Joanne, girl, I appreciate your concerns, and I know how you feel about relationship coaches, but I gotta do this for me, girl. It's all about me." I laughed, trying to lift the mood and change the direction of the conversation.

"All about you? That's the problem. We're still talking about you, and it's been like fifteen minutes. I just told you how stressed I am!" Joanne's polite tone had slowly turned into rage, with grunting and heavy breathing.

"Joanne, you called me. You started talking about your situation and your feelings, then you apologized. Then you went into talking about Ashton. I agreed with you about Ashton, and then

I let it slip out that I was here in Los Angeles, and you went on a rampage about why I'm here. I didn't have an opportunity to even ask you how you've been or check in because of the direction of our conversation. However, I am okay with no longer talking about me. I have about ten minutes. Let's talk about you, and then I can call you after the conference." I hoped that Joanne would really hear this and be okay with it, but I knew she likely wouldn't.

"Oh, so you weren't even gonna tell me about L.A.? Why?"

"Because of how you're responding right now," I said.

"Yeah, because it's silly that you're there, and you're by yourself. What the hell is wrong with you, Taneshia? Those guys aren't interested in women like you. They're looking for the Rihannas and the Beyonces of the world, not basic-ass women like us!"

"What? I am not out here trying to get with one of these guys. I'm here trying to get help! And I only have like an hour to get ready. Joanne, I really love you, and like I have said before, I really feel like we aren't on the same page lately, and I don't know how to get back."

"I do; we will get back when you start being the Taneshia I first met, who listens to me, who cares. Now, all you do is take flights, without me I might add, and go to codependency retreats and meetings. Okay, we're codependent … Damn, let it go! What are you seeking by going to all these things! We have to just ask God to help us and let it go!"

I listened to Joanne, and she sounded exactly like she did when I was at my dad's house a couple months ago. Even though I wasn't ready to let Joanne go in my heart, in my mind, I knew it was time. Our friendship had run its course. Between Ashton and Joanne, I felt stuck. It was like I was in a box that I couldn't get out of. Neither one wanted me to change because me changing no longer benefitted them. It didn't have anything to do with me. They didn't wish me well. They wished I would always be there for them, and I was no longer that Taneshia. "I think this conversation is important and either needs to be had later, after the conference, or face to face. I come back home tomorrow. Why don't we get together when you're free?"

"Nah, it's all good. Enjoy your conference. Let me know when my *friend* comes back."

I heard light sobbing on the other end and then silence. I didn't know what to do. I looked at my phone and saw I had an hour to get ready and meet Karol and Tisha on the first floor. I decided to get ready and leave this topic for reflection after the conference.

Tisha, Karol, and I had all purchased VIP tickets and were glad we did because there had to be at least 100 women in the VIP line and about 500 in general admission. As the staff checked our tickets, we headed to the VIP seating area. "Ooh girl, you see him? Girl, he is so fine!" Tisha exclaimed. She was referring to one of the relationship coaches standing by the stage, Ace Metaphor. I had never heard of him before; but I was eager to hear him speak about self love and healing. . Even though every man in the room was attractive, I was there to get help.

As I glanced through the auditorium, I noticed one thing: Every man was busy working. Some were authors, some were videographers, and others were speakers. All were dressed well, smiling, and based on how big their smiles were they seemed to be living their dream. They all appeared to be financially stable (I assumed), could definitely teach me things about life, and based on what I had read about some of the speakers, everyone had a relationship with God. I laughed to myself. *Okay, God, I see you. You are funny. So, this is the arena my man will be in—entrepreneurship? What is he? Is he an editor or coach? or maybe he is an aspiring author like me, and we can write and encourage each other. Not every black man is either taken, in jail, or a drug dealer like I originally thought. To have a man that can support me … What?! Okay!*

I sat in awe. I was now in the presence of everything I had written on my list. Every man in the arena was working hard, looking amazing, smiling, and speaking with intelligence. I was in heaven, mesmerized by what God was showing me. I knew He was showing me this because He wanted me to have faith and do what He told me to do: write my book and tell my story.

Suddenly, somebody hit me on my shoulder. "Taneshia, girl, where you at? Stay with us! You dazed out, thinking about your favorite speaker, Stephan, huh?" Karol smiled, referencing a famous relationship coach and Christian author I really loved named Stephan Labossiere. He was the reason I came to the conference. I had read his famous book, *God Where is My Boaz,* and it made me think about so many things. When I got the email about this conference, I wanted to come to hear more.

I chuckled. "Stephan is fine, girl; so is Ace. I see why you like him. But I'm here to listen to what they've got to say, girl! I need it. I've been taking care of everyone else for years, and now, here I am at thirty-five, trying to practice self-love with no guide on how to start.

"Ooh, Jesus!" Tisha hit Karol on the leg. "Girl, why Taneshia my twin healing sister?! Taneshia don't love herself, either, girl; that's why she's here!"

Damn! Well, I wouldn't say all that, but I guess so.

Karol looked at me. "Taneshia, you and Tisha kill me. Y'all are beautiful. Don't let this world tell you you're not."

"Thank you, Karol. I appreciate you and you as well, Tisha."

The lights grew brighter, and the speakers came to the stage. The first person to speak was Ace Metaphor. "Okay, okay … The show's about to start, y'all, and that's my pretend man up there." Tisha and I giggled softly at Karol's proclamation, and then we focused on the show.

"Welcome, ladies, to the Self-love Summit!" Ace said with enthusiasm. This is a space for us to talk, love, laugh a little, and support you on your healing journey. Is that okay? We've got some poets that will come during intermission and rap a little, and we're gonna have a good time!"

The crowd applauded in glee, ready to eat up all the information they had to give. As I listened to each speaker, I took notes in my journal, ecstatic about how intelligent the speakers were and the knowledge they shared. It was amazing to hear them. We sat there, laughing and healing and just having a great time. I still couldn't believe I was in a space of healing and meeting new people. And God had me covered the whole time because he had Tisha and Karol, both from the Bay Area like me, waiting to meet and bond with me, so I wouldn't feel alone.

Stephan came to the mic to end the summit. As he spoke, my pen was ready and my heart was open. "Before you leave tonight, ladies, I just want you to know that anyone who is truly meant for you will love you. You being yourself will not be too much. Your text will not go ignored. He will want to bring clarity to you, not confusion. But I encourage you to take this time of being single to heal and love yourself. Who are you? What do you like to do?

Are you in the best shape of your life physically and mentally? All these things are important when we venture into relationships. I pray for all of you that you do your healing work and allow God to guide you. If you're looking for specific information, my books are at the table to the left of you. I have a lot of helpful books that cover everything from healing to learning how to pray for your mate … everything you need. I love you all."

I stared at him in awe. I loved the message; it was so powerful. Every dime I spent to attend, I would have paid again. I never even thought about being in the best shape of my life. I had struggled with diabetes since I was sixteen years old and never thought about how that could impact my partner or my relationship. I wanted a child. Did I really want to put my husband through the ups and downs of wondering if his child and I were okay while I was pregnant due to my crazy blood sugar numbers? Hell no! My weight and health were areas I'd wanted to address in my life for a while. Stephan didn't even know God had used him to spark a match in me to take care of my physical health and make it a priority.

"That was beautiful," I said.

"Yes, it was, girl. You see I'm over here crying," Tisha said.

"You want to take a picture with him after the show and grab a book?" I said, hoping she agreed and would go with me.

"What?! Girl, hell no! We can order those books and get them delivered to the house. I ain't going up there; I'm scared."

"I am too, but let's go!"

"Nah, I'll take your picture, though."

I didn't know what to do. I was scared to go up there, but I was also tired of being scared. I had come almost 400 miles to hear him speak. Why not tell him what a great job he did and how

God used him? I was tired of being the Taneshia who thought she was unattractive and unworthy of using her voice. I was going.

I got up and walked through the crowd to get to him. To my surprise, only about seven women had managed to get in line before me. Stephan looked amazing as he took pictures and signed books. His long, neatly braided locs flowed down his back, and his beard was lined up perfectly. The red blazer he wore made his brown skin pop, and his smile reminded me of a rainbow. He was gorgeous, a man of God, and intelligent. I was scared to death to say anything to a man of his caliber, but I had to. I had to do it for me. Even though I had all his books, I decided to grab one for my aunt and Joanne. Perhaps it could be a way for her and I to reconnect.

Before I knew it, I was next in line. I gave myself a pep talk to encourage myself to speak, not just smile and take a picture. *Taneshia, tell him why you came. Tell him what God told you to do about writing a book. Speak up! He is just a man. He puts his pants on one leg at a time just like you. Breathe. You are worthy. You've got this, girl.*

As I opened my eyes, I felt an embrace on my shoulder. It was Stephan! "Hey! How are you? Thank you for coming."

Speak, Taneshia! Say something! This is your time! "Hi, Stephan. I loved your message today. This entire conference was amazing. My name is Taneshia. I'm from the Bay Area but had to come and hear you speak. I really needed it. I'm considering writing my own book, and what you said today really helped me," I said with a big Kool-Aid smile.

"Aw! That is amazing to hear. Thank you. I'm so glad you came. And you should definitely write that book if that's what God told you to do."

"Yes, I agree. May I take a photo with you and have you sign these two books for some friends?"

"Absolutely; say no more. Who should I make the books out to?" he said while taking them from my hand.

"One is for Joanne. And one is for Evelyn."

"Okay, got it," he said while writing out their names.

As he signed, I glanced over my shoulder, looking for Tisha. She was to my side, waving and giving a thumbs up, proud that I'd stepped out of my fear and talked to him. As she walked closer to me, I passed her my phone and looked at Stephan.

"Okay, you ready for the pic?" he said. "Where are we looking?" He placed his masculine, chocolate hand around my waist.

Damn, his hands feel good. Wow! I want to feel this every day, Lord. Hurry up and send my man ASAP. "Uh… uh … this way," I said, struggling to stay focused while his hands were on me. I took a deep breath and allowed myself to enjoy the moment. I stepped closer to him, making sure my body was relaxed and my smile was big. We both looked at the camera while Tisha took the photo.

"Okay, I got about three," Tisha said."

"Perfect!" Stephan said, smiling. "Congratulations on starting your book. Thank you for coming out." He shook my hand and handed me my signed books.

"Thank you, Stephan, so much! This was great. Have a great day, and God bless," I said and walked away.

Oh, my goodness! You did it! You did it! You talked to him. Yes! I was so excited to have stepped out of my comfort zone and done something I wanted and needed to do.

"You better get it, girl! You have earned that waffle at Roscoe's, girl!" Tisha laughed as we walked off.

Karol was purchasing books at another table. She waved at us as she grabbed her books from another author before joining us. "Did you get your picture, girl?" she asked me.

"Yes, I did," I said, smiling.

"Girl, she was so confident. She didn't look nervous at all," Tisha said.

"Trust me, I was. I had to give myself a pep talk and some deep breaths," I said, shaking my head.

Tisha, Karol, and I went to Roscoe's Chicken and Waffles to eat. We laughed and joked about the summit. Tisha raved about how fine Ace Metaphor was and how she deserved someone who treated her like she imagined he would, and I talked about my book and how I was ready for a change in my life. Karol smiled and advised both of us to live our lives and do what makes us happy. We left the restaurant feeling full, physically and emotionally.

When we got back to the hotel, we said our goodbyes, and I headed back up to my room. The day had been so good. Not only did I step out of my comfort zone and come to the summit alone, but I even met some amazing people who just so happened to be from the Bay Area. Even though I'd gotten into a little disagreement with Joanne before the summit, I was happy.

I decided to call my dad and update him about my list and the show. I grabbed my phone from my purse and dialed his number. It was about five a.m. in Tampa, but sometimes I could catch my dad up that early, running errands and starting his day.

The phone rang. "Hello, hello, Taneshia Johnson. Wow, it's late over there in California. What are you doing up at two a.m.?"

"Hey, Dad. I'm in Los Angeles at the conference, and it was awesome. Not only did I meet that author I was telling you about, but I met new relationship coaches that I gained so much information from. Oh, and guess what!"

"What, Taneshia?"

"I completed my list!" I said, shaking it in my hand, ready to tell him about it. "Dad, God is funny. I was thinking that everything I had on this list wasn't realistic, and boom! … I come here, and I see men working in their purpose. It gives me hope that maybe the things on my list aren't so unrealistic.

"Taneshia, say what? Are you serious, honey?" My dad seemed to be just as shocked as I was.

I laughed in agreement. "Yeah, can you believe it?"

"Well, you have to tell me what's on the list now! I'm too eager to hear. Matter of fact, do you have it written down? Send me a copy, so I can look along."

"Yes, I do. Okay, I'll email it to you now as we talk." *Wow! He really cares about what's on my list. He really cares about me.*

I was amazed to hear my dad seem so excited to hear something about me. I was starting to put everything together and discover that my dad had always loved me. Maybe I just needed to be more vocal about what I needed, so I felt like I was being supported.

"OK, I just hit the send button; you should get it soon," I said, relaxing on the big, fluffy bed and resting my head on one of the pillows.

"OK, let me go to my office. You know your old dad is slow. I was in the kitchen. It's gonna take a few steps, daughter, to get to my office." We both laughed.

"Take your time, Dad. It's okay." I said, stretching out on the bed, getting comfortable.

"OK, baby. I'm at my computer, getting ready to pull up this list here. Let's see, let's see, what you got here." When my dad repeated himself like that it generally meant he was excited. And knowing that he was excited about something important to me felt good in my spirit. My inner child was so happy, she was screaming, and it manifested into a huge smile on my face.

Suddenly, I heard my dad chuckling. "What's so funny?" I said, smiling curiously.

"Taneshia, this list is truly the list of a grown woman. I was thinking you may have some crazy things on here, but this is great. This list here is exactly the kind of man I would love to see you with. Someone who can listen and take care of you. You deserve that, sweetie. I look forward to walking you down the aisle one day."

Wow, he really does think of me. I can't believe it. I always thought he didn't care anything about me, and now here he is, talking about walking me down the aisle. I really have been reading his cues wrong maybe almost my whole life. I guess all it really took was me speaking up and not being afraid to tell him what I need. "Wow, Dad! That is such a beautiful thought. I look forward to that too."

My dad and I spent another hour going back and forth about the kind of guy I wanted. It felt like heaven, having him listen to me and support me. That's all we want at the end of the day. We want people to hear us, love us, and show us they care in the same manner that we show them. It sounds so simple yet seems so hard for us to get that from the people we go above and beyond for daily. Speaking our needs and having hard conversations is not easy; however, that feeling of comfort and warmth when someone is showing us they care is priceless.

I fell asleep that night feeling loved, valued, and wanted. It was some of the best sleep I had gotten in a while.

9

Transitions

I landed in Oakland feeling like a million bucks. I was eager to get home to start writing and planning out my book. I had never written a book before, but I had written twenty-to-thirty-page papers for graduate school in one week. So I knew I could easily write a book too. The problem was I didn't know what to write about. Should I write from a clinical perspective, since I was getting my therapy hours and may be a therapist soon, or should I write from my heart? I was scared to write from my heart because I would be admitting to the entire world that, for a minute, I thought I was going crazy. But maybe that was what God wanted me to do. It all felt so confusing.

I glanced through my phone and saw I had missed a call from the previous Friday. *Oh wow! How did I miss this? Who is this from?* I checked the message, and it was from the job with the

Department of Public Health. *Oh no … You know they only call you when you get the job. Did you really land that job, Taneshia? The one in the ghetto with kids throwing paper and Cheetos at your head? Ugh!*

I listened to the message, and, indeed, I had gotten the job. Patrick's voice was gleeful as he shared the news. "Hey there, Taneshia. This is Patrick from the Department of Public Health. I want you to know we have chosen you for the position. I am so excited for you! The combination of your personal experience living in neglected neighborhoods and your years of on-the-job experience made you the best candidate for us. Please give me a call so we can talk about a start date and all the details. Take care and have a great weekend."

Wow! I got it. Now what do I do, go to the ghetto every day to work? Possibly get shot up on the bus or while walking to my car? That's if I drive, because if I drive, I'll be sitting in an additional thirty minutes of traffic. Will my car even be able to sustain that type of wear and tear anymore? Can I go through that again?

Two things were happening for me: First, I was tired of not knowing what to do and feeling stuck; secondly, I was tired of doing things that were "best" for me or my social work career, which I wasn't even sure I wanted. I walked through the airport confused and upset. It seemed like the high I was on in Los Angeles had been snuffed out in the two minutes it took me to listen to that message. The clarity I once had felt like it was gone, and I was now left to decide whether to take a job I didn't want just to level up in a field I didn't know if I still wanted to be in.

I went outside and headed to the train. As I walked, I started crying. Life felt so complex, but one thing I discovered was that I was done doing things I didn't want to do. That part of me was dying, and even though I was happy about it, I was perplexed about the direction in which I wanted my life to go. I pulled out my phone and called my dad. He'd wanted me to call him when I got home anyway, and I could really use some words of encouragement.

"Dad, hey. I'm back, and I'm safe."

"Praise the Lord! Thank you, Jesus! How was the flight?" he asked.

"It was okay. Got some news about that job, though," I said with a sad tone.

My dad gasped. "What did they say? They want somebody with a license?"

"No … I wish! They're offering me the job."

"What? Oh, wow! Well, what are you feeling, baby? Are you happy, don't want it, what? I don't know what to say, you know?"

He is really trying to not only be supportive but be in tune with how I feel, so he can feel the same way and offer support. Maybe our calls were always five minutes or less because I was always waiting for him to say something. Now that I'm talking more to him, he's also talking more with me.

I was so taken aback by my dad's response that I almost forgot to respond. "Uh, well, yeah … I am kind of perplexed. This would be an opportunity for me to get my hours, but I'm just not sure about the neighborhood and hours of work, you know?"

"I know, sweetheart. I'm nervous too. I know you're grown, and I'm all the way out here in Tampa, but I just don't feel comfortable knowing you're gonna be in a bad neighborhood every day and there is nothing I can do about it.

So he would want to do something about it? Is he saying he wants to protect me? I reflected on other conversations we'd had in the past and could see clearly for the first time that my dad always had a desire to protect me. This was the first time he verbalized it but not the first time I felt protected. I guess it was easier to add up all the things he wasn't doing and proclaim that he didn't love me, telling myself that I wasn't lovable, versus looking at what he was doing. I decided I needed to stop having conversations in my head and just ask him.

"Dad, have you always felt this way?"

"Yeah. I mean, but what can I do? I asked your mom to move to Florida with me when you were younger. My divorce was final, and I was trying to step up to the plate and see if things could work out with her and me, but she said no for good reason. She probably sensed I wasn't ready to be in a relationship again. I was just doing it because of you. You know, to see if we could make things work to raise you together."

This was a story I had heard before when I was younger, but hearing it as a grown woman, I was able to empathize with my father and understand his point of view. "Yeah, I know. She told me."

"She did?!" he said, shocked.

"Yeah, she did. I guess it just wasn't meant to be. I never knew you had ill feelings about it, though. That's new to hear."

"Of course. You are my daughter, Taneshia Johnson. I love you."

I sat on a nearby bench because I felt tears swelling in the corners of my eyes. I tried to open my eyes to avoid crying in public, but it was too late. "I love you too, Dad. I'm headed toward the train station, but I'm going to call you tomorrow, okay?"

"Okay, Taneshia. Text me when you get in the door."

Text when I'm in the door? He really is concerned about my safety … "Okay, I will."

I ended the call, holding my phone in one hand and wiping tears with the other. Every word he said was ringing in my ear, and the message I got was that he loved me. He had always loved me. He just didn't know what I needed. Other people loved me too. I just had to overcome the thoughts in my head that told me otherwise and speak about my needs while understanding that they are human like me. They will mess up. They will not read every cue sometimes, but it doesn't mean they don't love me. My dad always loved me; he didn't show it the way I wanted him too, but he did.

Having a conversation with him about what I needed changed everything. I dreaded doing it at thirty-five, wishing I had done it earlier in my life, but I was tired of beating myself up. I was thankful to get the support and love I needed from him, even if I was thirty-five.

I found a piece of paper and a pen in my purse. I pulled them out and began outlining my book. The words came naturally and easily. I knew it was God. I thought about the journey I had been on from the age of thirty to now and decided that to really tell my story, I would have to share everything: the horrible experience I had in Las Vegas with my ex; my intrusive thought patterns; my issues with emotional eating; and my lack of boundaries. I suffered from a combination of depression and anxiety, all triggered by codependency.

I started writing from the beginning—how I felt at thirty and how I had pictured my life would be compared to what it actually was at that age. Ironically, Joanne was a huge support during those years. We would go to support groups together, talk about the Twelve Steps together, and heal together overall. It was so nice. I missed that version of her. This new version had forgotten all about everything we had learned, and she seemed obsessed with seeking love through sex and over-giving to men who didn't deserve her. She'd even had sex with a few women. I didn't judge her. I just noticed how seeking love had caused her to explore various avenues.

After writing about it a little, I realized that was what bothered me about Joanne. Even though she had found out about the twelve-step group before me, somewhere down the line, we parted ways. She was in a relationship—I wasn't. She was struggling in school and doing Uber Eats to survive; I graduated with a master's degree in social work and had a good city job. I guess, in a lot of ways, we were living completely different lives, and it hadn't hit me until that moment.

I took a moment to pause from writing and reflect … *Damn, Joanne and I are completely different now. What does this mean, though? Have we always been different, and I just couldn't see it?*

I continued to write. I started by writing about how I found out I was codependent, and then I moved to stories of Joanne and I attending our first codependent meeting together. In less than twenty minutes, I'd already written five pages! It was surreal. I looked at the pages and smiled. I couldn't believe I was writing a book.

I heard my phone ringing. It was Ashton. I was shocked that he was calling me. It was as if I had said nothing to him. I nonchalantly picked up the phone and put on a fake smile. "Hey, boo. How's it going?"

"Boo? That's still not the name you gave me before, but I guess I'll take it."

I remained quiet. *Here I was, putting on a front to be polite, and he was still talking shit and trying to control what pet name I called him.* I used my irritation to set a firm boundary once and for all. "Ashton, you know, I was thinking … I really enjoy our friendship, but I think it's best we no longer hang out as much, or kiss, or touch each other."

The phone was silent for a few seconds as I waited for his response. "What do you mean? I don't understand. Did you meet someone at that conference? Because you know those kinds of men like top-notch, dead-gorgeous women, right?"

Is this man calling me ugly? Calm down, Taneshia. Ask him what he meant. Don't assume, and don't go off. "What does that mean? 'They like top-notch, dead-gorgeous women'? I don't understand what you're saying."

"Baby, you are sweet, and that smile you have is gorgeous, but the men you're looking at just … I mean, frankly sweetie, they aren't in your league."

Yep, I was right. He is calling me ugly. "So, what I am hearing you say is you are assuming I went to the conference just to meet a guy. And in addition to that, I am not good looking enough to be with any of the men I met over the weekend? Is that right?"

"Wait a minute … When you say it like that it sounds bad. I didn't say all that."

"Ashton, that is exactly what you said. I may have paraphrased, but that's what I heard. Why don't you tell me what you meant?"

"Honey, you're blowing this whole thing out of proportion.

Ooh, okay. I see what is happening. He's gaslighting me like I'm crazy. "Okay, so now what you said isn't really what you said, and I'm crazy?"

"Baby, what? What are you talking about? Let's start over."

"Okay."

"All I'm saying is I don't understand why we have to change

anything we're doing just because you went to that event in L.A, and, by the way, you didn't even give me a chance to ask if you were back."

"I went to the event because I wanted to hear what the speakers were talking about. And, yes, one of my favorite authors was there. He encouraged me to start writing my book."

"A book? Baby, that's great! I'm so proud of you. Listen, I'm excited you're back. Remember, I haven't seen you in a while. Let's go to dinner tomorrow and talk more, okay baby?"

"I have some things to do this week. Let's catch up in a few weeks or so, once things settle for me."

"What? A few weeks? Baby, we haven't seen each other for almost three months."

"I know, and that's okay. Because we are friends. And like I stated before, I think it's best that we don't hang out as much. I treat you like a boyfriend. And it's not healthy for me. I don't wanna do that anymore. I should be dating men who are interested in me, who can love me, you know? I'm sure you want that for me, right?"

Ashton was stone silent on the other end. If I hadn't already realized it, this conversation revealed to me that he was a narcissist. "Yeah, yeah, of course, Taneshia. I mean, if you think that's best."

"Yeah, it definitely is. Well listen, I'm on the train, so I'll catch up with you later. I hope you have a great weekend, Ashton."

"Yeah, you too."

And just like that, the nightmare I had lived for eighteen months—being gaslighted, manipulated, and lied to—was over.

It was a new work week, and I finally made it to Friday. I had a lot on my mind. Between being excited about my book, the potential new job, and breaking up with Ashton, I felt good. And to make things better, I had my first therapy session with a new therapist. I hadn't told Dr. Jones I wanted to end sessions yet because I wanted to check out this new therapist first. I scheduled the session in the morning, while my mind was fresh and I was ready to talk.

Pulling up to the parking lot was a very different experience from when I visited Dr. Jones. For starters, it was much closer to my house, and it was in a nice area. I'd no longer have to pass homeless people or tents or clutch my purse when I got out of the car. Her office had an on-site parking lot. I already liked it. I got out of the car and walked toward the door. There were a few different businesses inside the building, but it was easy to find her door.

I walked in and a beautiful light-skinned black woman with glasses greeted me at the door. "Hi! Are you Taneshia? I'm Karen. It's nice to meet you." She extended her hand to me.

"Hi. Yes, I'm Taneshia." I shook her hand and walked into her office.

I sat on a blue couch that was once a turquoise color but faded. I glanced up and saw a bookcase with different types of therapeutic books on its shelves as well as some self-help books about drug and alcohol addiction. I set my purse on the floor, looked at her, and smiled.

"Well, it is really nice to meet you," she said, smiling. I noticed she didn't have her notebook out like Dr. Jones. I liked that. It made me feel like we were going to have a conversation, and I wasn't going to be diagnosed again.

"Yes, I'm so happy you had space," I said, crossing my legs, getting comfortable on the couch.

"So, what brings you to therapy?"

"Well, I know this might sound crazy, but I feel kind of split. I feel like I'm two people sometimes. There is one part of me that knows what I need and goes after it; then there are other parts that are really scared, codependent, and worried about losing people in my life if I say no or set boundaries." *It feels so good to be honest.*

"Okay, I see. Well, let's talk more about the codependency part. Is that something you concluded on our own, or how did that come about?"

"Well, see … I kinda already have a therapist …" I said reluctantly. "I have been working with her for about six years, and I feel we have either come to a fork in the road, or maybe I just need a different type of therapy for where I am right now. I will admit that I don't see her weekly like she recommends, so it really could be my fault for why I'm not where I need to be," I said, laughing, hoping it would prevent me from expressing my real emotions, which were sadness and depression.

"Mmmm … I see. Let's talk about that for a while. What do you think?"

"Okay, yeah."

"So, when you say it's your fault, you're referring to where you are in your healing journey, correct?"

"Yes, yes, I am."

"I wonder how the narrative would change for you if you gave yourself some compassion. Maybe everything you're doing and experiencing is all part of the work. Maybe you *are* where you need to be." Karen shrugged while looking at me for confirmation.

I smiled in delight. I never thought about it like that. "Wow!" I said in awe.

"Yeah, I mean a lot of people can't afford to come once a week, but it doesn't mean they aren't doing the work. It doesn't matter how many times you come. You come until things feel clear for you."

Until things feel clear for me … I really like that concept. Okay, Karen, I see you! You may have a new client, sis!

I felt an instant connection to her after that statement. The compassion and support she showed me was something I hadn't gotten from Dr. Jones in a while. Dr. Jones always pressed me about not coming enough, rescheduling appointments, talking to my dad, and she questioned me about Ashton. It felt like a lot. I knew it was all love, but I'd gotten beaten up enough in my relationships; I wasn't trying to pay $130 to get beat up by my therapist too.

"Right. Yes, I definitely see what you're saying, and I agree. I decided to seek out another therapist for a couple reasons: one, my insurance will pay for me to see you. Coming once a week is something I want to do, but I could never afford it with my current therapist. And two, you are closer. My current therapist is about twenty miles from my house."

"Yeah, both of those are not good. I understand." We both laughed. "I saw you're an MSW; I am too."

"OMG, what!? Karen, that is amazing. I am so proud of you! I tried to pursue my hours, but something always got in the way. As a matter of fact, my current job offered hours originally but then said they had to stop because the work wasn't clinical enough." I shook my head and shrugged in disbelief about my own story. I had forgotten how painful that was.

"Oh, wow, Taneshia. I'm so sorry. I know that must have been shocking."

"Yeah, it was. I just connected with how much that hurt me just now. I shrug things off like it's nothing. That's another thing I want to work on."

"Shrug things off ... Okay, let's talk about that. What does that look like for you?"

I love how compassionate and open she is. Catching every detail of what I tell her and helping me sort through my thoughts. "Well, often, people will hurt my feelings or say things I really don't like or do things I don't like, and I don't say anything. I just find a way to take care of myself. Most times, it's by eating and avoiding, but I'm working on that. Setting boundaries is still kind of hard. I mean, I can do it, but I do hesitate to do it, especially with people I don't know."

"Mmm ... that makes a lot of sense. It can be difficult to set boundaries in the beginning. It sounds like you have a high level of self-awareness about your own behavior pattern, which is beautiful."

"Thank you. Yeah, I guess I do know myself pretty well. I have been in codependent recovery groups for about six years at my church. We recently ended it last year, but I learned so much. I wouldn't trade it for anything."

"Taneshia, you have done some great work. I am honored to meet with you more. I have an opening next Thursday at four p.m. Would you like that?"

"Yes, I will take it."

"Perfect." We stood and shook hands. "I will see you next Thursday at four p.m., Taneshia. Today was a pleasure," she said.

"Yes, it was! See you next week. Thank you, Karen!"

I was so excited after therapy. I had finally met a therapist who was helping me bridge the gaps of my new self and old self.

Joanne and I were rocky, but with this new self-awareness about myself, I decided to call her. We always shared victories, regardless of what we were going through, and this was a moment to celebrate.

I dialed Joanne. The phone rang about six times before it went to voicemail. "Hey, sis! OMG, chile! I got another therapist, and she is the bomb! I am so excited. Remember when I was telling you I was gonna book with her? Well, I did, and it was amazing!" I chuckled. "Call me as soon as you get this. Love you. Bye.'"

I hung up and turned the key in the ignition. I was so happy; I had to call someone. *Hey, I'll call Dad.* I picked up the phone again and dialed my dad's cell phone number. The phone rang and rang. My dad was known for running errands all the time. I figured he was busy, so I left a voicemail message. "Hey, Daddy! OMG, do I have updates for you. So not only have I written five pages of my book, but I had my first therapy session with my new therapist today, and it was great! I think I'm gonna call that job and take it too. I guess I should be considering my future in social work, right?" I rolled my eyes while saying that. It didn't feel like the best work environment for me, but Karen reminded me that I did want to become a therapist. And gaining my clinical hours was the only way that was going to happen. My job no longer provided the hours, so this was the best move, the smart move. "Dad, I don't wanna leave you a long message, but I love you. Call me when you can."

I drove back home on cloud nine. I knocked my Soul for Real album in the car, dancing and grooving to every word. I was ecstatic. God had chosen to turn a new leaf in my life. It felt good to be gaining control over who I was and what I needed, no longer bound by my codependent patterns or negative thoughts. I was rediscovering who I was, having hard conversations with family and friends, and spending time loving me. I was even venturing out, meeting new people, trying new things, and considering sharing my story with the world. I didn't have a title for my book yet, but I knew as I continued to write, God would reveal it to me.

I finally made it home, and as soon as I did, I began writing. I grabbed my notebook, looked out the window, and took a moment to pray. "God, every word that I write in this notepad, let it come from You. In your Son, Jesus's name, I pray. Amen."

As I wrote, I cried. I couldn't believe I was telling people about what happened with Shawn in Las Vegas. I had friends who didn't know the details of that story. I was still in shock and sadness about him abandoning me in a hotel room. Shawn was an ex-friend, whom I assumed loved me and was considering being in a relationship with me. That night in Vegas made me realize he never felt that way about me.

There were a few reasons I wanted to leave this story out of my book, but I couldn't. If it wasn't for Shawn doing what he'd done. I may have still been codependent. That experience woke me up. I was able to finally see that something was wrong with me. Why would I get on a plane and fly out to see a man I had only seen a handful of times over a five-year period? Yes, we'd talked on the phone, and I felt safe with him, but I really didn't know him. I didn't know anything about relationships or love back then, so I was oblivious to the fact that he wasn't into me. I was embarrassed by the words I typed, but they were the truth, and God told me to do it.

I heard my phone ringing. It was Joanne. "Hey, sis!" I said, happily answering.

"Hey, girl, hey!" she said. "What are you doing?"

"Girl, I'm sitting here writing this book," I said, smiling and proud of myself.

"What? Still? You really doing that, Taneshia?" There was hesitation in Joanne's tone.

"Yeah, I am. Remember, I told you. I was thinking about it like three months ago while I was visiting my dad in Florida."

"Thinking about it and doing it are two different things."

I wasn't surprised by Joanne's response, but it was still disappointing. I decided I was going to ignore the negative vibes I was picking up from her and continue telling her my story. "Yeah, girl, I'm really doing it. It's crazy you called now because I was just writing about Shawn."

"About who? Shawn? That fool! What the hell does he have to do with your book? You're supposed to be over that!"

I was hurt by Joanne's response and was starting to feel insecure about my story. "Uh, yeah, I know, girl. But I have to. If it wasn't for him, I wouldn't have even realized something was wrong. My relationship with God grew; my emotional eating became real to me; I started going to the codependency groups; girl, I started healing! That's a major part of the story. I can't tell my full truth without it, girl. Don't worry, I am not ashamed of it anymore. I've prayed about it."

"Like you prayed about getting on a plane to go to a conference without me? Or like you prayed about confronting your dad about your relationship, which I feel was silly. Bringing up old shit from years ago, now that he's in his early seventies and just needs you to love him … Yeah, okay, Taneshia. You seem to be only thinking about you nowadays. Fuck the rest of us. Then got the audacity to say God said it was cool."

Joanne's manipulative and aggressive tone seemed to be the new way she communicated with me for the last three months. I was done with it. I had hinted to pausing our friendship before, but now it was time. I had tears in my eyes, and my throat felt like it was about to close. "Joanne, that's it, girl. I need to pause our friendship for a while. I am done. I can't do this anymore. The manipulation, bringing up old shit, the criticism … This isn't tough love from you anymore; this feels like straight anger and jealousy.

"Ooh, ain't nobody jealous of you, sis! Jealous of what? You're thirty-five years old, and just now living your own life. You still hate your job; you still struggle to set boundaries; you're still dealing with Ashton's dumb ass; you can't even see the man is playing you. So, tell me exactly what I am jealous of, Taneshia."

Okay, you wanna put your big girl drawers on today, Joanne? I'mma tell you about yourself … Nah, it's not worth it. Just leave it alone. End this friendship and be done. She's been like this longer than three months, Taneshia; it's been about a year.

"Joanne, I'm not gonna sit here and go blow for blow, tearing you down like you are doing to me. I appreciate the journey and the friendship we have had, but until you can talk to me with sense, love, and respect, don't call me anymore. Have a good night." I hung up the phone without even giving her a chance to say anything because Joanne was the type of person who always had to have the last word. I had learned during my recovery years that I didn't need that type of energy.

I sat on the edge of my bed and let my tears flow. I glanced at the clock: it was 7:15 p.m. in California, meaning it was 10:15 p.m. in Florida. Sometimes my dad stayed up until about 11 p.m.

I hoped it was one of those nights. I hadn't called him late like this in a while, but it was worth a shot to see if he was up to just share some time and vent with him. I picked up my phone and dialed my dad's number. The phone rang, and after about two rings, someone answered, but it wasn't my dad. It was my stepmom, Vanessa. "Hey, Taneshia. How are you, sweetie?"

"I'm okay." I was confused about why she had my dad's cell phone. I assumed he was already asleep. "Dad must be asleep. I hope I didn't wake you," I said.

"No, you didn't wake me, baby. You didn't get a call from anyone in your family?"

I raised my eyebrow, trying to figure out why someone would call me so late. "Uh … no, no I didn't. Should they have called me about something? I'm confused."

"Taneshia, your dad had a stroke yesterday. He's recovering okay, but he's in the hospital. I just got home from being with him all day. I'm bringing his cell phone to the hospital tomorrow. Give him a call then."

I was stuck. Couldn't speak. The tears I'd shed about Joanne were just a light rain before the storm that flooded my face. I wailed, unable to say anything.

"Taneshia, Taneshia, honey, it's okay. He's struggling to move one side of his body, and his mouth is a little droopy, but he is okay, honey. It's okay, Taneshia."

I just cried, rocking myself back and forth on my bed.

"I know, baby," she said, trying to comfort me. "Everything has been happening so fast. I apologize for not calling you. I was hoping your grandmother or aunt would have called you before me, but they're probably still trying to gather their thoughts too. We were eating breakfast, and suddenly, your dad started coughing, then choking and pointing to his mouth. He couldn't talk. I had to call a neighbor to take him to the hospital. Call him tomorrow, okay? I will make sure the phone is with him."

I took a deep breath and wiped my tears with my hand. "OK," I said and hung up the phone.

I lay on my bed, curled up like a crying child. I was in shock about what was happening to me. I had just seen my dad three months ago and he was fine. I didn't understand. "Lord, what is happening?" I looked out the window at the stars, trying to understand how I could lose my friend and find out my dad had a stroke all in one day.

I knew healing would be hard, but I thought I was more prepared for the storms of life. For these past few months, it felt like every step I made was knocking the wind out of me. I was anxious and afraid to live a life free from codependency, but I had to because I was tired of living with depression. I wiped my tears away as I cried, wrapping myself in a sheet. I looked up to the sky again and prayed. "God, I finally found my voice to speak. Please give me an opportunity to do it. In the midst of all the chaos, give me the strength, Lord."

I'd been suffering from a combination of depression and anxiety, and I was finally learning to be free and take the necessary steps to love myself and do what made me happy. At that moment, my book title came to me. I said it aloud to myself: *When Depression and Anxiety Have a Voice.*

I cried a few minutes longer, feeling a combination of happiness and pain. I wished I could call my dad and check on him, but I had to wait until the morning. I glanced up at the sky one last time before drifting off to sleep.

PART
3

Reconnect with Yourself and Your Needs

10

Finding Myself in the Meantime

I t was hard to sleep the previous night. Thoughts of losing my dad and regrets for not living closer ran through my mind all night, preventing me from sleeping. Every thought I'd had earlier that year felt stupid. *Maybe Joanne and Dr. Jones were right. Was I wrong to bring up that conversation with my dad so late in my life? His life? Maybe I should have just let it go.* I didn't want to waste time in my thoughts. I decided to pick up the phone and call my dad.

"Hello, hello, is this my daughter, Taneshia Johnson?"

I held back tears and cleared my throat. "Yeah, Dad, it's me. Lord Jesus. How are you? I didn't even know you were in the hospital!"

"It's okay, sweetheart. It happened quickly, you know? But I'm stable now. It's been a couple of days here now." My dad's voice sounded different, as if he had a lisp. I assumed this was what

Vanessa was referring to when she told me part of his face was a little droopy. "They tell me I will start occupational therapy soon, so I look forward to that. It's hard to lift my arm."

I paused, not knowing what to say, and shook my head as if my dad could see me. "Well, I love you. I am so glad you're still here. You need to slow down, Dad. You do a lot of running around."

"Yeah, yeah, I know. I guess I do need to take it easy. This stroke taught me that. It's a lot, you know?"

"Yeah, I can imagine."

"Lord Jesus, it's seven a.m. there; are you on your way to work?"

"I don't know if I'm going to go, Dad. I'm really not feeling my job, and with you in the hospital, I can't really focus on work."

"Taneshia, listen to me. Go to work, baby. I am in the doctor's care. I'm fine."

"I don't know. Should I go?"

"Yes, go. Call me when you get off, okay?"

"Okay, I will. Love you."

"I love you too, Taneshia. Bye bye."

I sat on the edge of my bed. My dad said to go to work, but I just wasn't feeling it. I sat there thinking about my life and started assessing myself. As I healed from codependency, I found strength in seeing myself evolve. I had come to realize that healing from codependency required five things: self-awareness, self-acceptance, self-forgiveness, an obligation to self to change, and creating a plan for change that is realistic. I was happy that I saw myself in the planning phase but sad because I was struggling to determine what that looked like for me.

I sat there confused, in pain, and with no desire to move. I was getting tired of things going well but then declining in my life. What happened to that beautiful journey people told me I would have? When I was going to therapy, coaching sessions, and my twelve-step group, I heard beautiful stories of the love, peace, and hope I was supposed to experience. Instead, I was confused, hurting, and exhausted from telling people what I needed and how to treat me. Part of me knew this part of life was required in order to grow and heal. I had to learn how to adapt to change and not allow others' responses to impact me. But I also felt it should've been easier than this.

I looked at the clock and saw that it was close to eight a.m. I was supposed to be at work in thirty minutes. Considering I still hadn't taken a shower or gotten ready, I figured it might be best to notify my supervisor that I wasn't coming in. Five years ago, I would have gone in out of guilt and obligation, saying things to myself like, "Taneshia, your clients are counting on you," or "Taneshia, you have such a good job," or, my favorite, "Taneshia, its only eight hours." But it didn't matter. What mattered was my feelings and taking time for myself to focus on what I needed, which, in this case, I wasn't so sure of.

Making decisions for ourselves as codependents is one of the most difficult things to do. We have a history of knowing how to put others before ourselves, therefore we don't have much experience reflecting on our own needs and wants. Even though I was still unclear about what I needed, I was very clear about what I didn't need. I knew I had no desire to go to work and hear other people's problems for eight hours of my day. I wanted to be alone with myself and my own thoughts and get support for the next move I needed to make to get through this hump life was giving me. Tears began to swell in my eyes. Instead of holding them in or shaming myself for crying, I just allowed them to fall. This was not what my life was supposed to be like. All the years I had spent in search of what it meant to heal from people pleasing had seemingly resorted to even more pain.

Am I going to lose my dad now? Will I be a daddy-less daughter emotionally and physically?

I got up and looked at my phone. I thought about the job offer I received. Did I really want to take it? Images of kids throwing Cheetos and balled up pieces of paper at my head ran through my mind. The idea of dodging bullets, breaking up physical fights, and seeing people struggling to survive daily made me sad. Yes, in many ways, I signed up for this type of work as a social worker, but I was seventeen years in the game. Was this where I deserved to be at this point in my life, at thirty-five? Who was I kidding? As a 5'8" plus-sized woman, how many times could I run to my car or the bus in one week without getting tired or getting robbed or hurt? There would always be that resident who didn't like a comment I made and might be waiting for me after work. Then what would I do? And besides all that, I just didn't want to do it. That should've been enough not to take it. My current job was no longer giving me clinical hours, but did I really need them? Did I want to be a therapist? Or did I just want to be a bomb-ass master-level social worker who supported people through my writing?

I grabbed a tissue from the side of my bed, got on my knees, and prayed. It was hard at first because I was sad, angry, and disappointed by God about my father being sick, the job, and everything that led up to this point. I looked up to my ceiling and said, "Lord, I am so sad. I am so distraught. I honestly don't know what to do. And You know I don't have anyone to ask but You. So here I am. I hate my current job, and I can't seem to get a leg up. No one has called me back about another position, except the one I don't want. Do you want me to be a therapist? Tell me, please." My tears grew bigger and dripped to my chin. I grabbed another tissue, blew my nose, and continued. "Lord, I need You to tell me what to do. Please. I don't know. I just don't know. I feel like with every step I make, I get knocked down. Is this what you really want for me, a life of pain? I don't believe that in my spirit, but every situation that comes up feels like this is the hand that is being dealt to me. I love you. Amen."

I ended my prayer because, at the end of the day, I could ask God to tell me what to do all I wanted, but God does not physically speak to us. But I'd forgotten that the feeling in my heart that kept telling me not to take the position was God speaking to me. I decided to lean on my faith and call Patrick. I scrolled through my phone and found his number. As the phone rang, I wondered if this was the right decision. No one answered, so I left a voicemail message. "Hi, Patrick. This is Taneshia Johnson. I interviewed for the clinician position a couple of weeks ago. I have decided it is not a good fit for me at this time. Thank you so much for considering me, and I hope you find the candidate you deserve and need for your department. Thank you." I hit the end button and took a deep breath. "It's over. Thank you, Jesus."

I pulled my curtains to the side and looked out the window, smiling about the decision I made. But I was still in pain about the confusion in my life. I couldn't believe that now that things were finally turning around, my dad was sick. I didn't know what my next steps were, and I was afraid to think about it too much because it brought up an unmanageable sadness that had been trapped inside of me for years.

I reached for my laptop and started writing my book again. I wrote the title that God had given me the night before, *When Depression and Anxiety Have a Voice,* and envisioned what to write about. I had originally started with sharing about my journey of learning I was codependent. I also wrote about Shawn and Vegas, but now what? What was next? I went through so much during that time, and I had blocked a lot of it out to keep me safe and avoid thinking about it constantly. I guess the next thing was to share about my moments of depression.

Jesus, this book is gonna be hard to write. God, you really want me to tell people this stuff? Even though I thought I was crazy for admitting this stuff to people I didn't even know, I trusted that God would make sure it got to the hands it needed to get to. It was my mission to write it and let Him do the rest.

Before I knew it, I had been writing for almost two hours and had completed another twenty pages. It was such a liberating feeling to get all my trauma, feelings, and emotions out on paper. It was like painting a picture with every color I could think of at my fingertips. I didn't know anything about writing a book, but it looked like I was writing one. I figured I'd better try and find someone who could edit it for me. YouTube and I were best friends. I decided to search YouTube for videos about the requirements for writing and publishing a book. To my surprise, I found a lot of videos of authors giving tips. Apparently, two big things I needed were an editor and a book cover designer. Some authors recommended a marketing team and social media manager, but those things were irrelevant for me. I just wanted to find someone who could edit my book, and I had to find a graphic designer for the book cover.

After about two hours of watching countless videos about various authors' processes for publishing their books, I grew tired. I grabbed a bite to eat from the kitchen and took my plate back into my room. I had just seen Dr. Karen a few days ago, but considering everything going on, I decided to reach out to her to ask if I could see her before our upcoming scheduled session. Staying in isolation is never good for those who are healing from codependency. We tell ourselves we don't need help, things are okay, and we have everything under control, but I was in a state of full transparency with myself. I wasn't okay. Life felt unmanageable, and I needed support to get me through. Not only was this okay to do, but it showed my growth.

I picked up my phone to call her. "Hey, Dr. Karen. How are you? This is Taneshia. I was wondering if we could meet again earlier this week."

"Yes, yes, of course. Hi, Taneshia. Is everything okay?"

"Well, I just found out my dad had a stroke and figured I should take care of myself. Normally, I hold things like this in, but that really isn't healthy. I am trying to stray away from that."

"I hear you, and I am glad you reached out. Actually, I had a cancellation today. Could you come in this afternoon around five p.m.?"

"Yes, I can!" I said, elated she could meet with me so soon.

"Okay, great. I will see you then."

"Great! Thank you so much."

I glanced up at the clock and saw it was almost noon. Setting boundaries and speaking up for myself always made me tired. Between finding out my dad was sick and turning down the job, I was exhausted. I decided to take a nap until it was time to get up and go to session with Dr. Karen.

I got up and started getting ready for therapy. I pulled some black leggings out of my closet and a t-shirt and hopped in the shower. As I washed my body, tears streamed down my face. I had let go of the idea of hiding my tears from myself or others. My life was just sad, and it had to be expressed. When we don't express our true feelings to ourselves and others, we end up minimizing our inner child. That inner child is sad, disappointed, and confused. We need to allow ourselves to feel all the emotions we are experiencing without shame, and that's what I was doing by releasing my tears. I was happy for the moments of joy I had experienced, but the moments of pain—setting boundaries, saying no, and speaking up for myself—were drowning me.

As I drove to therapy, I went over what I wanted to talk to Dr. Karen about. Dr. Karen and I really didn't know each other yet, but she seemed easy to talk to. I got a calmness and an empathetic vibe from her that I enjoyed. I decided that even though our therapeutic relationship was new, I was going to share my real feelings and thoughts with her. I needed someone to help me put all the pieces together. I needed answers for some of the decisions I made and next steps to feel better.

Why the hell did I let Ashton into my life? And why is Joanne flipping out now that I am truly trying to heal? What is that about? Is it me? Is our entire friendship just a joke? Does she really care about me at all? I needed insight from Dr. Karen. I pulled up to the parking space and gathered my purse and sweater from the car.

I pulled the door open and walked into her office. "Hi, Dr. Karen," I said, sitting on the couch and placing my purse next to my feet.

"Hey, there. How have you been? I am so glad you reached out to me."

"Yeah, I had to. It's been … kind of heavy this past week."

"Mmm … Yeah, say a little more," she said, crossing her legs and grabbing the cup of coffee next to her. She took a sip as I gathered my thoughts.

"Well, last week, when I came and saw you, I kind of told you just a glimpse of how I really feel. I was hoping, today, I could share more." I was nervous as I spoke. I had talked to only Dr. Jones for almost six years now. Telling a stranger how I was doing and being honest about it still felt surreal. I grabbed some tissue from my purse because I knew I would start crying. I was tired of crying, but I also accepted that it was part of my healing process. "Well, the year started off crazy. And even though I'm sad my dad had a stroke; he is a big reason I am where I am now."

"I see. And where is that, Taneshia?"

"Alone, always second-guessing myself, and not knowing my worth. I watch him and his wife tell stories of living well while my mom and I suffered. It's been like this since I was a child. But because he has now had a stroke and he's old, I have to forgive and forget." I felt my face getting warm as tears streamed downward. "It's just fucked up. Excuse my language, but I don't know any other way to explain it. Then, after being left in a hotel room in Las Vegas a few years back, I was abandoned again earlier this year by my friends. I was supposed to be going to Las Vegas at the beginning of this year with my friends to celebrate my birthday, but everyone flaked on me. Some put more effort into their excuses than others, but they were all bullshit. We had been planning that trip for months, and they all made a conscious decision not to come. But I know things come up. I'm just in my feelings right now," I said, wiping my eyes. I looked up at Dr. Karen and realized I had released a lot in just a few minutes. "I'm sorry. I know I've said a lot and I am all over the place."

"No, that's okay. It is my job to help you make things make

sense. You just focus on being present for yourself and speaking your feelings like you're doing right now." She wore a look of compassion and kindness that I hadn't seen in a long time. It felt comforting. I wiped the tears from my face, blew my nose, and continued.

"You know, when I was in my early twenties, I had thoughts of being married with kids and even having a dog, even though I'm scared of dogs." We both laughed. "I don't know what happened to that dream. When I was diagnosed with depression and anxiety a few years ago, everything shifted for me, and when they told me I was codependent, life did a 180-degree turn that I don't think I have fully recovered from yet. I think this is another part of healing for me that I don't know what to do with. The first part was somewhat self-explanatory: go to therapy, go to the twelve-step group, find a coach, and repeat. But what about after? Now that I have completed the twelve-step program, been to therapy for six years, and worked with a coach for a year, what's left? I find myself being so focused on setting boundaries and trying new things, and it feels great, but this year was a year of advocating for myself and my needs, and I watched everything crash." My tears overpowered my voice as it began to tremble. I just sat there, disappointed from hearing my own story aloud. My eyes were fixated on the floor, and I occasionally looked up at Dr. Karen.

"Wow, Taneshia! Can we process a little bit of what you shared?"

I nodded, still too shaken up to speak.

"Taneshia, I want to be honest and say I don't quite know where to start in terms of what's happening for you, but I will say that completing a twelve-step program to heal from codependency is huge, and having a consistent relationship with a therapist is awesome. It is exactly the outcome many people want on their healing journey. So, congrats to that! Secondly, let's talk a little bit about the disappointments from this year. I heard you say the year started off with you being abandoned and alone. Is that how your friends made you feel, like they abandoned you?"

"Yes. I mean it was my birthday, and they know I don't really have any family in California."

"I see. Where is your family?"

"In Georgia and Florida."

"I see. So your friends are more like family to you?"

"Yes, very much so."

"I also heard you say you spent time with your father earlier this year?"

"Yes, I did."

"Share more about that."

"I went to see my dad the second week of January. And even though none of my friends could go, I still went to Las Vegas on my own. I wanted to have fun before I had the hard conversation with my dad about how I feel about our relationship. It was hard. My dad and stepmom don't really understand how hard my life has been and still is at times. They have money and resources; I work for everything. I *have to* work for everything. You know my stepmom didn't even bother to call me and let me know my dad had a stroke? She told me she thought my family would have called. Are we not all family? What kind of comment is that to say to someone who just heard their father had a stroke? You see what I mean? It's just messed up."

"Right. Like what does that mean, 'your family'? Did she not marry your dad? You all are family!" We laughed.

"Right, OMG, Dr. Karen, yes!"

"I kid … But seriously, what I am hearing, Taneshia, is you don't feel seen by the people that say they love you. And I think the losses you have experienced this year have really made it clear to you that you no longer want to have the same narrative. You are setting boundaries and speaking up, and it sounds like, as a result, your relationships are shifting in ways that you don't feel prepared for."

Wow, she is good. This is only the second session, yet she has my number. It feels good to be heard. I cried and nodded. "Yes, yes …" I said, fighting to speak through my tears. I closed my eyes and allowed myself to cry.

"Taneshia, if you could have one thing at this moment what would it be?"

That is a powerful question. I want so many things. I don't even know where to start. "Wow, that question Is fire." We chuckled and Dr. Karen passed me tissues from a box close to her. I grabbed them and continued. "At this moment, all I want is to live my own life without guilt and shame. I want to be okay with people leaving my life. I want to be okay with the decision I made to tell my father how I really felt, and I want to give myself the love I gave away for so many years." I wiped my tears with the tissue, this time taking off my glasses so I could wipe my entire face.

"That is a powerful statement you just made, Taneshia. You are so deserving of all those things. What are some ideas you have for beginning to live in that moment?"

"I guess I could let go of the guilt that keeps me down about my dad and friends. There is one guy friend I had named Ashton. He told me we were special friends. But the whole time he was using me for emotional support while he dated other women. But I was so broken when I met him … All I knew was he was a man who wasn't physically hurting me or verbally abusing me. I didn't realize it was emotional abuse until about eighteen months in."

"And thank God you did," Dr. Karen said. We shared another laugh.

I liked her. She had a different, low-key, down-to-earth style that I really enjoyed and needed at this time on my healing journey.

"Taneshia, I kid a lot, but my feelings for you are sincere, and I hear what you are saying. I am wondering if perhaps we could talk a little about Ashton. If you are codependent, and it sounds like you know for sure you are, it is highly possible that Ashton is a narcissist."

Yes, yes! Say less, sis! He sure the hell is! I nodded again in full agreement. "Yep, hands down, Dr. Karen, he is. I looked it up, and every word I read described him. It was crazy! I have been healing for almost six years now; how could I have missed it."

"Well, I think maybe the question is how could you have *seen* it, right? The behavior he demonstrates as a narcissist is normal for what you have experienced in the past. You have been healing for six years but codependent for thirty-five. Do you hear the variables in that scenario?"

I nodded.

"So, I think the question is how could you have seen the signs? And in addition to this, what did you do to see the signs, because whatever that was, it's working well for you."

"Wow, you just flipped that whole thing. I feel all grown-up and proud of myself." We laughed.

"Well, you are," she said, smiling.

"Well, what I did to be able to see the signs was start reading more books about codependents and the seemingly magnetic attraction to narcissists. I have also been working on setting boundaries, not doing things I don't want to do, praying, seeking a new therapist—which I found in you—oh, and I went to a self-love summit with all male relationship coaches, and it sparked me to really see the type of man I want and deserve. My dad and I had put together a list of the type of man I want, and when I went to the summit, that's all I saw. Isn't that crazy?"

"Yes, and another thing that is crazy is you sitting here saying you haven't done any work and not giving yourself credit."

I was happy but also confused. *So, is this healing? All the madness that's happening to me?* I decided to ask. "So Dr. Karen, if I'm hearing you correctly, you're telling me that this is healing. This is what healing looks like? Feeling like I am losing the ground under me and I don't have a foundation to stand on?" I was really trying to figure it out, because I was starting to get irritated with myself and my entire life experience.

"Yes, that's exactly what I'm saying, Taneshia. This is healing. Working through the hard times in life and coming up with a plan. And what you have come up with so far, my dear, even though it may feel hard, is exactly what you should be doing." Dr. Karen smiled at me.

I glanced at the clock and saw we had gone ten minutes over. Dr. Jones had been strict about time. We had gone over just a couple times, and even then, she made sure to tell me we were going over. "I'm so sorry, I went over my time," I said, gathering my purse.

"No, that's okay. I wanted to make sure we talked about this fully before you left. How do you feel?"

"I actually feel good, I mean really good. I haven't felt this good in a while. Don't get me wrong, I am probably going to cry in my car and more when I get home, but at least I have some tools to work with. I know this is part of the journey, and I can stop second-guessing myself and just be in my emotions."

Dr. Karen clapped in excitement. "Yes, that is the spirit, Taneshia!" We both stood. "Are you a hugger? It just feels appropriate to give you a hug after this session. It was tough."

Am I a hugger? Hell yeah! Wow, she is nothing like Dr. Jones. I can count on one hand how many times Dr. Jones has hugged me in six years. "I am a big hugger and could definitely use one," I said, extending my arms. We hugged, gave each other pats on the back, and walked to the door.

"I have a slot open now for this day every week. So, I will see you weekly now, right?" she said while opening the door.

"Yep, I will be here," I said with a smile.

I headed toward the car, feeling a mix of emotions. Even though I was happy, I was still sad. It was good to know that this was healing, but I was also sad because I didn't know what or who else would leave next. I got into my car, turned the ignition, but stayed in park while I prayed. "Lord, this session was great. I think I have finally found a therapist that gets me. I ask, Lord, that the questions you want me to reflect about come through her. She asked me some good questions today, and I know they came from You. I thank You, Lord, for this opportunity to see a therapist and not have to pay so much money. Thank you, Lord, for consistency and just being able to talk to someone about how I feel. Lord, please continue to be with me. Thank You, Lord, for my dad being okay, and continue to be with him and the doctors caring for him. I love You. Amen."

PART
4

Repair and
Unlearn

chapter

11

Finding Peace at Rock Bottom

As I got up from my bed to take a shower, I looked in the mirror. Dr. Karen and I were meeting weekly, and our sessions were going great. I was building a relationship with her that was taking me to areas of healing I had never experienced before. Even though things were at a standstill in my life, I was finding contentment with being uncomfortable. I was still writing my book, still hating my job (yet going every day) and finding peace with losing relationships with people. Saying no takes you to a place of isolation that brings peace. It doesn't feel like it at the moment, but it does. I wish I could explain it, but it is something everyone must experience individually.

I went through the daily routine I'd been practicing for the last month: take a shower, put my hair in a bun, put some clothes on that somewhat match, and drive to work. I remembered this pattern well from my depression days. I used to judge myself for feeling depressed and felt like I had to do something. These days, I was learning that it was okay to not be okay. Taking a daily hard examination of my life helped me stay humble and develop a deep level of self-compassion. I flipped through my phone and found my favorite playlist that included songs by Mary J. Blige, Tasha Cobbs, and Fred Hammond. I allowed it to play at random until my favorite song came on, Tasha Cobbs' "He Knows My Name." I sang along as I contemplated calling my dad. I was going to be sitting in Bay Area traffic for at least an hour and a half, so I figured why not.

I dialed my dad's number, hoping he'd answer. "Is this my beautiful daughter, Taneshia Johnson?"

I smiled. I loved my dad's enthusiasm. It was funny to find purpose in everything he did now. I silently cried to myself, wishing I'd recognized these things about him earlier, instead of feeling angry.

I cleared my throat in hopes that it wouldn't sound like I had been crying. "Hey, Daddy. How are you feeling? Did you go to physical therapy today?" I asked, hoping he had already.

"Yep, yep. You know it's eleven a.m. here. Those classes are at nine a.m., which I'm happy about, daughter, because they're not easy. I'm trying to get the movement back in my left arm, you know?"

"Yeah, I remember you telling me that last week. Does it feel a little easier to lift?"

"Just a little easier." We both chuckled. "Taneshia, I am just thankful to still be alive, you know?"

"Yes, yes, I know. I'm happy too, Dad. So, I was thinking … You're going to be released from the hospital soon, so I should probably come visit when they say you can go home, right? I know you and Vanessa are gonna need some help. I know we talked about this already, but since it's closer to release time, I wanted to mention it."

"Taneshia, I think that's a great idea. There is no point in you sitting here next to me now. Your grandmother and Vanessa do that every day."

"Right, my thoughts exactly."

"How are you, baby?"

I didn't know what to say. *Should I tell him I have a new therapist, I'm losing friends, and I still hate my job?* I just didn't feel like those were things he should be hearing just after having a stroke. I decided to share a little but keep it brief. "Well, Dad, it hasn't been good for me. I've been really worried about you, still hating my job, and my best friend may possibly no longer be my best friend." I took a deep breath. Just speaking it aloud felt heavy.

"Wow, baby. Lord have mercy. You're talking about Joanne?"

Taneshia, your dad is a rockstar! He remembers her name. "Yeah, yeah, Joanne!" I said in disbelief.

"Lord, you guys have been friends a long time. Is she still dealing with the same young man, or does she have another one?"

Either I've been talking too much or my dad has a good-ass memory. "Nah, it's a different one. This one has a kid."

"What? And she's dating him? She doesn't have kids, right?"

"No."

"Wow! Well, baby, sometimes we outgrow folks. It's an old saying that goes when people start leaving your life: It's just God preparing you for new people. So get ready, Taneshia. Hey, maybe a young man is coming. Remember your list! We prayed over it, so it will be."

I cried, listening to my dad. I was so happy we had these times together. It was what I'd been praying for all along. I grew quiet as the tears ran down my face. "Yes, it will. I believe that too."

"And as for the job … It might be time to move on, daughter. I was shocked when you said you weren't happy. I wasn't expecting that; you've always loved social work."

"I know. And certain parts of me still does. Helping people is my passion. I just don't think doing it in this setting is fitting for me anymore, you know? Maybe you know, because I don't," I said, hitting the steering wheel with my palm in anger and hopelessness.

"Yeah, I know it's hard, baby. Just hang in there. Our Father in heaven knows and will take care of you."

Prior to me talking to my dad in this way, I used to think he said these things because he didn't want to help me figure out what to do. That was me viewing the situation as that six-year-old wounded little girl, not the grown woman I was. I was slowly learning that my dad didn't know how to guide me, but he knew God would, and that's why we talked about prayer so much and even prayed with me. Accepting his love language brought peace to my heart. The thoughts that previously told me my dad didn't care or didn't love me were fading away as I allowed myself to be loved by him.

"Thank you, Daddy. Listen, I can go on and on about how tragic my life is, but I am not gonna do that while you're healing and recovering. I love you. Get some rest, and I will call you when I get off, okay?"

"Okay, baby. One last thing …"

"Yes, sir?" I said.

"How is that book going?"

"I'm almost done. Can you believe it? I'm currently looking for an editor. I looked up requirements for getting a publishing deal; it's not worth it, and it's hard. Then some people want like two thousand dollars to help you advertise your book. Plus, I would still need to find an editor and graphic designer. So, I've been searching YouTube, and it looks like I can publish it myself. So that's what I'm gonna do. Now, I just have to find someone to help me."

"I am proud of you, Taneshia Johnson. If anyone can do it, you can, baby."

Listening to my dad speak so highly of me and my capabilities made me realize he had always thought of me this way. That was why his friend in Tampa already knew about so many of my accomplishments. He was proud of me. He was proud to be my dad. He wasn't ashamed like I thought. Perhaps in the beginning, when I was born, things were hard. I could imagine co-parenting across the country would be hard for anyone, but I could see how my dad did genuinely love me.

My dad and I told each other "I love you," and I hung up the phone with a smile.

I pulled up to the office, found a parking space on the side of the building, and prepared my mind to go in. I reluctantly grabbed my bags and purse out of the car and walked toward the office. As I pulled the doors open, I pushed the second-floor button for the elevator, saying hello to the security guard at the door who was pretending not to be asleep. Per usual, I had a big smile on my face and a big hole in my heart. I just had no desire to do the work anymore and couldn't seem to get my zeal back. I looked down at my clothes to find I had put on yet another all-black outfit. I know it seems unbelievable, but most days, I didn't even know what I was putting on. I just checked to make sure it matched, it was clean, and it was something I could still fit.

I got off the elevator and walked to my desk to find coffee and red roses. I was confused. Who had done this and why?

Ooh, maybe I have a secret admirer? Did that cute author at the self-love summit do some research and find me? Maybe he said, "Let me brighten this beautiful black woman's day and send her flowers."

But I sat at my desk only to read a note from Ashton. *How did he even get this up here?*

I heard heels clacking, coming toward my desk, and I turned to see one of my coworkers. "Taneshia, OMG, this cute guy dropped these off today with security. When I heard who they were for, I offered to bring it to you. Who're you dating that you didn't tell me about?" she said, smiling, sipping her coffee.

"You like roses? 'Cause you can have these. I'm just gonna throw them away."

"Throw them away? What? Who sent them?"

"Girl, that fool Ashton! This ain't nobody new. He's not even mine. He belongs to any half-decent looking woman with a vagina. He is a liar and a narcissist that I allowed to waste eighteen months of my life," I said while tossing the coffee and note in the garbage can.

"Damn, Taneshia. You mad, huh? What happened, you used to love him?"

"A version of me that didn't feel lovable loved him. I am no longer that person," I said, passing her the roses.

"Oh, okay. Well, thank you. You know I love roses. How is your book going?" she said while sitting at my desk.

"It's going pretty well. I need to take time today to find an editor."

"Uh, Taneshia, I can tell you are on one this morning, but did you see there was a note in here?" she said while pulling out a small envelope from the trash.

"Yes, I threw it away on purpose. It wouldn't be Ashton if it wasn't some lying-ass note in there about how much he misses me and loves me, and how I'm his 'special friend,' blah blah blah, girl," I said while turning on my computer and grabbing a notebook and pen.

"I think you should at least read it, Taneshia," she said, handing me the note.

I snatched the note from her hand with a fake smile. "Thanks, sis. I will." I tossed the note on the side of my desk while looking at her.

"Oookay," she said while taking another sip of coffee.

"I'm sorry. I was already feeling a little down after talking to my dad this morning, and then I come to work and see this crap on my desk. It's not a good start to my day, you know?"

She held my hand in agreeance. "Taneshia, I know things are hard for you. Your dad is sick, the whole thing with your friend, and then turning down the job ..." She shook her head to empathize. "It's a lot, friend. Well, I don't wanna keep you, but know that I am here."

"Thank you." I stood and gave her a hug.

I sat back down, glancing at Ashton's note. *Ain't no need in opening it; you know it's some bullshit, asking you to come back to him. Don't forget this man pretty much told you that you are ugly and no other man of higher caliber would want to be with you.*

I sat there in silence, listening to my thoughts, questioning why I even wanted to open it. I picked the note up, ripped it into small pieces, and threw it back in the trash next to me.

I picked up the phone to call Ashton.

"Oh, my goodness. My day is going to be amazing now because I heard from my baby. Hi, baby," Ashton said. His voice sounded cunning and manipulative to me now. The rose-colored glasses I'd been wearing when it came to him were gone, and I could see the devil he was.

> *As we heal we get more in tune with our inner thoughts. We learn to stop dismissing behavior and see things in true form as they are.*
>
> **@Tjselfcare**

"Hi, Ashton," I said plainly.

"There we go with that 'Ashton' shit again, ugh. OK, I guess I will have to just allow you to call me that. When are you going to call me teddy bear again?"

"Ashton, its early. Let's just have a real conversation this morning. Here are a few boundaries I need to put in place with you: Don't bring me gifts; don't send me gifts; don't text me or call throughout the day, and when and if I decide to see you again, let's try our best to be cordial, with no physical touch."

"Wow! Who is this calling me because this isn't *my* Taneshia. You OK?"

"I am great. I haven't felt this good in a long time," I lied, looking down at the floor, trying not to cry. Parts of me wanted to cry, to tell him to pick me up after lunch and explain how stressed I'd been with my dad and my life. There was a part of me that knew after good food and kisses and someone listening to me, I would feel better, but I had to shut it off. That was a younger version of me who never had anyone to listen to her or give affection when hard times surfaced. And even though I had empathy for "Little Taneshia," I had to put sis in her place because it was over with Ashton.

"Well, you sound irritated," he said.

"I am! I am irritated that you don't respect my boundaries!" I looked around to see if anyone was listening to me.

I walked outside because I could see this conversation was triggering for me. Once I got outside, I sat on a bench. "Ashton, listen to me when I say I am so, so good. We haven't really talked in a little over three months, and I have been floating on a cloud. You don't know how to be a friend. You act like a boyfriend and then try to play me like I'm crazy. I am so done with that and with you. Let's just be cordial when we see each other in the streets and move on."

"Move on? Wow, OK. If that's what you want."

"Yes, I really do."

"Okay. Well, have a good day. I have to go."

"Okay. Yeah, you too."

It felt good for it to finally be over with him. I walked back inside smiling. It didn't surprise me that Ashton didn't fight for me. There was no begging, no pleading, just the end. Parts of me felt sad and wanted to call him back, but I knew better. This was another confirmation that he was indeed a narcissist, only focused on his own needs. And since he couldn't get what he wanted from me anymore, he was done.

Knowing what I knew about narcissists, I gathered that Ashton wouldn't even bother to contact me again. But just in case he did, I would be ready to let his ass know, again, that it was over, and the consequence for attempting to cross my boundaries would be excommunication—no access, "don't even speak when you see me" type shit.

I checked my calendar and realized I would see Dr. Karen later. "Thank you, Jesus," I said while looking down at the notification. I definitely needed to see her after all of this.

I began scrolling through Instagram. I had been following the hashtag #blackauthors for a few months and started reaching out to other authors on Instagram to see how they'd published their books. Sometimes people responded to me with good information and sometimes they didn't respond at all. This time, instead of asking authors if they had time to share their experience, I decided to be more forward. I was tired of my self-esteem impacting decisions I made in life. My plan was to go ahead and state via direct message exactly what I needed help with, which was editing.

I found one author I decided to reach out to. I saw she had a book about domestic violence and depression. I figured since she and I were writing in the same genre, she may have been able to help. I hit the direct message button and typed the following: Hi, my name is Taneshia. I am an aspiring author. Congratulations on your book. I am curious to know how you went about finding an editor and publishing assistance? My manuscript is almost complete, and I am confused about the next steps. Thank you in advance.

I finally did it! Just came out and asked for what I wanted! Yes!

It is important to note that the version of us that is afraid to step out and try new things is our wounded child. It will remain this way until we do the work and take the necessary chances to paint a different image. This will require us to try new things, gain new experiences, and make new attempts to do things we have always wanted to do for ourselves.

To my surprise, I got an instant reply from the author. She informed me that I needed to find an editor that supported me in copy editing and developmental editing. I had no idea what she was referring to but continued to read her message. She directed me to a woman named Monique Mensah, sharing with me that she had lots of experience and would be a great fit for me as a first-time author. I typed a thank you message while beaming, ecstatic that she offered to help me and I was finally stepping out of my box, doing something *for me.*

I saw some of my coworkers walking past me, smiling. I was sure they were wondering why I was grinning so hard. God knows they hadn't seen a smile like this on my face in years. Even though things seemed to be falling apart in some areas of my life, I remembered what Dr. Karen had told me. She said *this was* healing. Perhaps the fantasy I'd had in mind that life would be all roses and sunshine once I healed from codependency was wrong. Maybe it looked exactly like this: ups and down, trials and tribulations, good times and bad. But in every case, the difference was I was there for me, and I was finally putting my own wants and needs first.

I took an hour or so to research Monique. The first thing I wanted to see was if she was an author also, so I searched for her name on Amazon. I had come across so many people and agencies that were running scams, and I didn't want to take the risk of wasting time with another. I saw on Amazon that she had written five books and had hundreds of reviews. She had even won awards for her books. Sis was a big deal! She had also posted pictures of herself with other authors at different events. I was impressed and felt excited about the possibility of working with her.

I searched her name on Instagram. After a few scrolls, her name popped up on my feed, and I scrolled through her page. She had posted several videos about how to publish a book, editing, and even how to market books. It was like discovering a gold-mine. I clicked one of her videos to hear what she had to say and determine if she was a good fit for me, and she was. I loved her zeal and confidence and knew she would be the perfect person to help me publish my own story. I listened to her in amazement. She was beautiful and confident; not to mention, she was a black author herself, who had written five books and sold thousands of copies. She was someone I needed.

I sat at my cubicle, feeling happy for myself. I was finally making moves based on what I wanted to do in my own life, not what people told me I should do. I was researching something for *me*. It felt good. I didn't know who I was. I had become a woman who was putting herself first at all costs. I kept hearing Dr. Karen's voice in my head, and I concluded that this was healing. We know we are healing when we can manage hardships in life and still center ourselves and our own needs. And that's exactly what I was doing.

I went to Monique's website and saw she had an opening later in the day for a consultation. It was perfect. She had a time slot right after my therapy session. *Yaaaass! Thank you, Jesus!* I smiled and danced at my desk. I am sure some of my coworkers thought I had officially lost it, or they were questioning whether I had found another job. I didn't care. I was taking care of me, and it felt so good.

I glanced at the clock and saw that I had less than two hours to get to therapy. I called a few clients, wrapped up some notes for work, and proceeded out the door. I knew what type of traffic awaited me and didn't want to risk being late.

I approached the therapy office with all kinds of thoughts in my mind, trying to organize them before I went in but decided I should allow Dr. Karen to support me and stop trying to do everything on my own. I grabbed my purse and sweater and walked toward the door.

I saw her standing there talking to another therapist while waiting for me to enter. "Hey there. How are you, Taneshia?"

I smiled, excited about what may be in store for today's session. Dr. Karen was beginning to surprise me with all her great insight, and I was eager to see what she had to say today. "I am doing okay. Better now."

"I'm glad to hear it. Let's go to my office." She pointed toward her door and we both walked in.

As always, I glanced over the office before sitting down and placing my purse on the floor. I was still getting used to the adjustment of sitting on a couch and not in a recliner. "It was a journey. Let me tell you."

"Yeah? Let's take some time to unpack that," she said while grabbing her coffee and crossing her legs. I liked that I was learning Dr. Karen's cues. One of Dr. Jones's cues was picking up her notepad and writing. Dr. Karen didn't write in her notebook during the session. I kind of enjoyed it; it made me feel more comfortable, as if I were having a conversation with a close friend, not being diagnosed and assessed. Everyone had their own style, but I enjoyed hers.

"Well, I must say the good news first. My dad is doing really well after the stroke!" I said with a big smile, clapping my hands. "And today, I think I might have found an editor for the book I want to write. I don't know who will buy it, but I want to write one."

Dr. Karen had a smile on her face but also looked concerned.

"What … what happened?" I asked, confused about the look on her face.

"Nothing happened, per say, but I am wondering if we can go back to a statement you made. One, that is amazing, Taneshia, about your dad, and writing a book is a huge accomplishment! Of course, someone will read it! What makes you feel people will not want to read it?"

I shrugged with a nervous grin. "I don't know. I mean, I'm not a real author, you know? I am just a girl from the projects telling my story about feeling like I'm crazy." We both laughed. I enjoyed the bond I was making with Dr. Karen. It almost made me forget I had to break the news to my other therapist that I wasn't coming back. It had been about two months since I'd even spoken to Dr. Jones. The fact that she hadn't reached out to see how I was doing was concerning. But at the same time, I could imagine my inconsistency with appointments may have made her feel like I was either done with therapy or had found another therapist, anyway.

"I think it may be time for me to tell my other therapist I want to end services with her. I guess that's the right thing to do, right?" I said, confused.

"Oh. I thought maybe you had already contacted her. I think that would be a great idea if you'd like. I think it would be good for you to get some closure. Six years is a long time to work with someone. I know, as a therapist, I would like that closure."

"Yeah, you're right, Dr. Karen. I'm going to call her. I really enjoy our sessions. I need help trying to figure out who I am. Sometimes ..." I paused, reluctant to make the statement aloud. I had never told anyone my true thoughts about how I felt about myself. "I ... I feel like I am two people. There are parts of me that really want to live my own life, set boundaries, say no, not care what other people feel or think, and just live and be. Then there are other parts of me that are terrified of doing that." I took a deep breath, nervous about Dr. Karen's response, yet also relieved to have shared that with someone.

Dr. Karen took a sip of her coffee before replying to me. "I can definitely understand and empathize with you. What are some things you have been experiencing that make you feel like that?"

"Just everything, you know? For every area of my life right now, I am making changes. I know you said that this is healing, but it sure does suck," I said, using my shirt to wipe the tears from my face. Dr. Karen passed some tissues to me. I blew my nose and continued. "Today, I officially told Ashton I was done. You and I talked about him being a narcissist, and I could see so clearly while interacting with him today. The control, the manipulation. It was crazy!"

"That is awesome, Taneshia. I can imagine it was difficult at the same time."

"Yeah, it was, but it didn't feel as bad as I thought it would. It felt like I was … like I was taking care of myself. I have been feeling like that for a while, and it feels really good. I am excited about where I am right now."

"You have every right to be. You have done some amazing work, Taneshia, and it sounds like this is just the beginning." We smiled at each other.

I looked down at my phone to see an hour had passed. "Oh wow, it's been an hour."

"Yes, yes it has. With everything going on right now, Taneshia, I am really happy we have a weekly routine."

"Yes, I am too. OK, perfect then. I will see you next week."

We both stood and shook hands. "Great! See you then."

I smiled while walking out the door. I felt good after each session with Dr. Karen. The clarity, by itself, was a game changer. I walked to my car with a bit of a strut, just in awe of myself that I was gaining an understanding of what this portion of my life was all about.

I heard my phone ringing and rummaged through the dungeon I called a purse to find it. I pushed my wallet, lotion, and other items I had forgotten about aside and found my phone, lit up and ringing, at the bottom. It was Monique, the editor I had found on Instagram! I unlocked the car so I could sit and be fully present for the call.

"Hey, Monique! How are you? This is Taneshia!" I said in glee. "I can't begin to say how happy I am you called. I am almost done writing, and I have no idea what I am doing. I have never written a book before," I said with pen and paper in hand to take notes.

She laughed. "OK, well, hopefully you'll want to work with

me, and you won't have to worry about that. Let me explain what I do. As you know already, my name is Monique Mensah, and I am a self-publishing consultant and an author myself. What I do is help you self-publish your book by doing everything for you, such as editing, layout, cover design, and publishing your book through Amazon and IngramSpark."

It was like she was speaking another language, but I was all for it because she let me know she could help me. "That is exactly what I need because I am so confused."

"OK, well, how far along are you with your book? I know you mentioned you were almost done."

"Yes, I am. I have maybe like two chapters left. I am sharing my story of being diagnosed with depression and anxiety and dealing with it."

"Oh, wow! That is so brave of you to share your story with others. If you want to move forward with me, I can send you my contract for services as well as an invoice, and when you have completed your manuscript, you can email it to me. In the meantime, if you'd like, I can take a look at a few pages and edit them for you so you can see how I work."

What ... she is gonna look at some pages now? This is amazing! "Okay, yes. I would love that. I will email it to you as soon as I get home, and yes, please send me the invoice and contract to go over."

"OK, great! It is going to be a pleasure to work with you, Taneshia."

"Yes, it will. Have a great evening."

"You too. Bye!"

"Yaaaaassssss!" I shouted in my car with raised hands.

I was so excited. The day had been awesome. I set firm boundaries with Ashton; my dad started physical therapy; my session with Dr. Karen was another eye opener; and to top it off, I had found, not just an editor, but a self-publishing consultant that could help me with everything I needed for my book! It was just a blessing.

I had a thought to call my dad. I remembered I had promised him I would call him when I found my editor. I had a lot of beautiful updates to share. All the good news could even lift his spirits.

I started driving home while calling my dad on speaker, smiling so big just knowing the news I had to share. I was in a completely different mood from this morning. The phone rang without an answer. I assumed my dad was asleep. I glanced at the time in the car and saw that it was seven p.m. in Florida. Perhaps he had decided to go to sleep early.

I hung up with the thought to call him later. I turned on the radio and grooved to some jazz music, snapping my fingers and moving my hips left to right. Life was good. I was on a cloud and didn't want to come down. To heal from people pleasing and codependent ways, we must begin to define what it looks like to love who we are and identify our own needs. This level of self-awareness opens doors to love, peace, and, finally, our own lives.

In this moment, I saw myself living my own life. It felt good to be who I was. I truly felt like I was taking care of myself. I was practicing saying no and being successful at it. The guilt and shame I used to feel five years ago was 99.9% nonexistent. It was amazing.

Before I knew it, I had pulled up to my apartment. I parked the car, got out, and did a little dance while walking up the steps. Once inside, I took off my shoes and clothes and prepared a bath for myself. I wanted to emerge my body in water and bask in the essence of the day. Everything felt so good.

I placed a bath pillow in the tub and added bubbles. I slowly lowered each part of my body in the tub and grabbed my loofah. I lay back on the pillow, still smiling and in awe of the amazing things that had happened during the day. I saw myself reclaiming power over my life. Dr. Karen had given me a lot to think about, and I realized that this was really healing—the ups, the downs, managing life, and even feeling like life is unmanageable. It was all me doing the work.

As codependents and people pleasers, the automatic response we often have is to do everything the right way the first time. If things start to get chaotic, it's because we didn't do something right. The goal is to always be in control; that way, we can't be hurt by anyone. I was learning that wasn't true. Living by someone else's standards will never equate to being in control. I thought being helpful, quiet, and supportive all the time was good and kept me safe from other people abandoning me. However, I was finding that those characteristics, without boundaries, are a setup for abandonment. I was attracting people who took advantage of me and left me when I set boundaries. The very thing I worked so hard to avoid—being rejected—was happening anyway. And there was nothing I could do about it but find a way to take care of myself and continually tell myself that when things fell apart, it wasn't my fault. It was just life, and I would get through it.

As I lay in the tub, I reflected on Ashton and how he came into my life like a tornado. He picked me up with his charm, sense of humor, and emotional support, and then dropped me like old garbage when I set boundaries with him. The idea of me living my own life was too much for him. The goal of the narcissist is similar to our goal as codependents. They don't want to be rejected, either. To avoid being hurt, the narcissist preys on people they feel need their attention. They seek out people who appear to have low self-esteem, low self-worth, or are going through hard times because they can show up like the superhero they pretend to be, loving, kind, and supportive … only until they build trust with us. After that, it's all about them, their needs, their desires.

Out of the eighteen months I had known Ashton, I could only recall the first six of them being about me. After that, it was all about him, and me doing everything I could to keep him and his love. Narcissists know that people who have low self-esteem and low self-worth will do everything and anything they want them to do. That's why they choose those types of people. And that is why Ashton had chosen me. He saw me at the bar that night with my wig on crooked, glasses barely hanging on my face, looking like a fish out of water. He had spotted me and my depression and was drawn to it like a moth to a flame.

I sat in the bathtub, smiling and crying at the same time, just taking time to thank God for the direction in which I saw my life going, and my ability to get out of that toxic relationship. Going to the Self-Love Summit was one of the best things I could have done for myself. It helped me see the reality of the real world around me. There were single black men in the world who weren't on drugs, in jail, or married. I just had to believe that I deserved one of them. I had shamed myself my entire life, saying I was too fat, too dark, and not lovable. After all, if my dad didn't love me, no man would love me. But now, it was like someone had removed the blinders from my eyes, and I could see how all those things were lies.

More tears came, and I didn't try to stop them. I held my

knees and thanked God for finally being able to see the gorgeous woman I was. I was loving myself, getting out of all the toxic friendships and "situationships" I'd found myself in. I was no longer taking the crumbs of life. Now, I was making my own moves, and everyone else had to follow suit.

I got out and wrapped a towel around myself and sat on the edge of the bed.

I saw a text from my sister: Call me when you can, dad isn't doing well.

Before I could start dialing her number, I heard my phone ring. It was my dad. I picked the phone up, shocked that he was still up; it was almost ten p.m. there. "Hey, Dad! Oh, my goodness, I am glad you're okay! I got a text from Laruen saying you weren't doing well. I have so many updates for you. I don't know where to start."

"Hi, Taneshia. This isn't your dad; this is Vanessa."

"Vanessa … Oh, hey. What's going on? You okay? Is Dad okay? I got a text from Lauren saying he wasn't feeling well. Did physical therapy go OK today?"

"Taneshia, your father had another stroke today. He is okay, but he can't talk. Some family and church members plan to come tomorrow and this weekend. I wanted to let you know. Can you come this weekend to see him?"

"This weekend? Well, I mean, is he gonna be okay? I was saving my time to come when he got home to help you both out for a couple of weeks."

Vanessa was quiet. I knew that wasn't good. "Taneshia, we aren't sure of your dad's condition right now. The doctors said this stroke was pretty hard on his body. I don't know when he will be coming home. I called your sister, and she mentioned that she is coming down, and I think you should too."

"Oh … oh, okay," I said, stuttering. I didn't know what was being said or what was happening. I was struggling to process what it all meant. My dad had another stroke? Was he okay? Could he survive another stroke? My knowledge of strokes was limited. I could do nothing but listen to her and cry.

I cried for most of the night, confused about what was happening and what I was experiencing. Isn't this how things always seem to work out? As soon as we begin to get clear about our life and find a way to cope and live, things change, and we find ourselves right back at square one, wondering how we are going to survive another hardship. That was me, struggling to understand why God would allow me to have only six months of pure support, love, and guidance with my father, only to take him away. What had I done to deserve this? As many of us are, I was a martyr by nature. I gave and gave and gave some more to anyone in need. Now, while I was in need, I felt I had no one. And, to my surprise, even God seemed to abandon me. I knew that wasn't true, and my inner child was just hurt, but I couldn't seem to gather any positive words of encouragement for myself. Life felt cold, lonely, and unapproving of any progress I was trying to make.

Eventually, I fell asleep with tear stains on my face, wrapped in my towel and wondering how I was going to continue life.

12

The Various Layers of Healing

After a six-hour flight, I was back in Tampa. I followed the crowd to baggage claim so I could grab my luggage and get a rental car. I had tried my best to find a flight for the weekend but ended up coming on a Wednesday. My family spent the weekend with my dad. I had gotten an update from my sister that our father, indeed, could not talk, but he was alert and eager to see her. That made me feel good, knowing he was alert. I didn't know how the doctors could help him talk again, but I had heard of people having strokes before and recovering after some time. I hoped that would be the case for my dad.

I started down the escalator and couldn't help but remember seeing my dad waiting for me at the end of it. Earlier this year and every time I came to visit, my dad was always waiting at the end of the escalator with big arms and an even bigger smile. I glanced at the empty wall he normally would be resting on and started crying. It's funny how you take things for granted in life. Things don't mean anything until they do, and by that time, it feels too late. I wondered if I was silly for going back and forth with myself about my dad and claiming to be so independent, not needing him at the end of my visit with him. Even though we had talked about it and were on better terms now, I still wondered what my experience would've been like with my dad if I had just said nothing and enjoyed our time together.

It felt surreal that he wasn't here to pick me up. Doing everything by myself was different. I had no idea where the rental car department was in Tampa airport. I never had to get one before because my dad was always there. After glancing around a few times, I gave up and decided to ask someone.

As I got the keys to the car and walked out to the parking lot, I thought of my dad. It seemed that with each step, I saw his face and remembered a moment we shared. I couldn't believe I was really going to see him in the hospital after another stroke.

Driving down the freeway ramp felt weird. I never realized how winding the road was. "Wow," I said aloud, gripping the steering real harder and hitting the brake. *Okay, which way do I go? Shit!* I hadn't turned on the GPS. I shook my head in disappointment. It was already dark outside, so it was just me and God.

On this first night, all I wanted to do was rest. I had reserved a room at the Hilton to get a good night's sleep and get my head together. I loved my family but didn't want to see any of them just yet. I was confused. Just driving around in Tampa was foreign to me. I didn't realize how much my dad had taken care of me in that way. I had focused so much on the things he wasn't doing well that I couldn't see what he *was* doing.

I managed to find my phone and type the address to the hotel into my navigation system. It was ten miles away. *Okay, cool. I won't be driving too far in the dark. I'm kind of hungry, but I'm not stopping at night. So it looks like the chips and water I have in my suitcase will have to suffice for tonight.*

I finally arrived at the hotel, tired, sad, and becoming more and more aware of how my dad used to take care of me, how all these little things were his way of loving me. Always picking me up from the airport (even though I was thirty-five years old), going to my favorite restaurant after I land or having food prepared for me at home. It was all his way of showing love.

I walked inside the hotel with my suitcase in one hand and my purse in another, remembering how my dad would take my suitcase. My whole mind was taken over by memories. It was like a puzzle I had been trying to solve my entire life, and now, life had released all the pieces I had been looking for. I was heartbroken, though, because it was at the expense of my dad.

I checked in and got my room key. I had everything I needed, so I wouldn't be leaving my room until morning. I opened the door, turned on the light, and took a deep breath. The bed looked so good. It had been a long flight and a long week preparing to get here. I knew I would be seeing my dad the next day and wanted to get some rest. I also wanted to reach out to my mom, so she'd know I was there. I picked up my phone and called her and decided to text both Vanessa and my grandmother to let them know I was in Tampa and safe.

I went into the bathroom and took a quick shower before lying down. I was happy my dad was alert so I could talk to him. I didn't know if this was going to be the last time or not. I didn't know much about strokes, but I was here and thankful to share another moment with my dad.

I jumped up the next day at nine a.m., got dressed, and checked out of the hotel. Vanessa had texted me the address to the hospital and told me she would meet me in the lobby. I drove to the hospital, valeted my car, and eagerly walked in. I thought of what I wanted to say to my dad. I didn't know who was still there from the previous week, but I wanted a minute alone with him.

"Hey," I said as I hugged Vanessa.

"Hey, sweetie. How was your flight?"

"It was okay. Long though. I didn't have a layover; it was a straight six-hour flight from California to Florida." We both shook our heads and laughed.

"Oh yeah, I know you're tired," Vanessa said.

"I am a little. I got some okay rest last night. I thought about Dad a lot. Where is the elevator? What floor is he on?" I said desperately.

"Taneshia, let's sit down for a second before we go up. I want to share your dad's condition with you."

"Condition"? What does she mean by "condition"? Oh, God ... I shook my head in confusion. "Condition ... I ... I'm sorry, what do you mean 'condition'?"

Vanessa held my hand. "Taneshia, your dad has been in a light coma for a few days. They had to put a tube in his stomach to feed him, and he hasn't really woken up from it yet. Your dad is older, so they are telling us it may take some time for his body to recover. Seeing you may be what he needs to wake up. Your grandmother is up there as well, and one of your cousins."

I paused, holding back tears. "Okay," I said, even though I wanted to say so much more. I knew the more I talked, the faster my tears were sure to come. It's funny how things work out. Over the weekend, he was alert and would've known I was there, when I couldn't get a flight. And now, he was unresponsive. I felt so betrayed by God. How could all this be happening to me? How come I always had to be the black sheep of my family, the daughter who was hidden like a gem under rocks?

I had to conclude that this was all in God's plan. And God's plan was one I had no right or privilege to inquire about. All I could do was hope He would show me a glimpse one day and make sense of what I was experiencing now.

Vanessa and I headed toward the elevator, and she pushed the third-floor button. As we walked out, I felt myself getting scared and anxious about my dad's condition. I followed her as she guided me to the room. We went down the hall, which felt like forever, until we finally stopped at a room toward the right. I saw my grandmother, cousin, and my dad. He was connected to tubes to help him breathe, relieve himself, and eat.

"Hi, sweetie," my grandmother said.

"Hi, Taneshia," my cousin said.

As they both got up to greet me, I stared at my father, unable to speak. I glanced at my family, angry and hurt because I wasn't told earlier about his condition. I decided this wasn't the moment to show any negative feelings; it wasn't like they would be able to help me process them anyway. So, I said hello and gave them both a hug.

I stood at the edge of the bed in a daze, placing one hand on my dad's leg.

"Jay Jay, look who's here, Taneshia Johnson," my grandmother said softly in my dad's ear.

"He has been like this for a couple days now," my cousin

said. "The doctors can't really say what's going on, so we just pray and wait."

Tears sprung from my eyes. "I've got to go! Oh, my God!"

I ran out, rushing to what I hoped would be someone's arms to embrace me and tell me I wasn't living this nightmare. But there was no one there, so I ran to the window, looking up at the sky, talking to God. "No, no, no … Why? Why, Jesus! No … No!"

I couldn't believe this was happening. I couldn't believe I was watching my father take his last breath. All the work I had done to heal and be able to tell him what I needed had gone to waste. It felt like I had wasted precious years, holding back what I needed from my dad. What if I'd told him two years ago, five years ago? I would have had more time with him, bonding and loving each other like we'd been doing these last six months.

A big part of healing from codependency is understanding that things aren't our fault. When things go wrong, it's not because we are bad people or undeserving. It is the way of life. Our job is to gain an understanding of what we need, while also being joyful that we are finally aware of our own needs and wants in life, no longer only thinking of others. Even in the storms of life, we find that we can find balance by understanding it is okay to have needs and feel our own feelings. We don't have to be perfect.

I was still trying to find the blessing in this moment, but I knew beating myself up for not telling my dad how I felt years ago wouldn't make me feel better and it wouldn't change anything. I didn't want to waste more time arguing with myself. I decided to go back to the room and spend time with him and my family.

"Taneshia, honey, are you alright? I thought Vanessa told you about your dad's condition," my grandmother said, looking at my stepmother.

"I did tell her. I don't know what happened. I guess it was too much," Vanessa said.

I glared at her, unable to hide my disgust and disappointment from her comment. "Uh, yeah … It is too much!" I yelled with tears still falling from my eyes. "I'm literally watching my father struggle to take each breath and, ultimately, maybe even die! I don't care what anybody says to me; there is nothing in the world that can prepare anybody for this. Y'all have been watching him for weeks. I literally just got here twenty minutes ago! So, yes, this is definitely a lot! The whole situation is a lot. I hear about everything after it has already happened. So, yeah, it's *a lot*!"

Calm down, Taneshia. Breathe. Breathe. Apologize for your tone and language. It is clear they don't understand how you feel. It's not fair to blow up at them. You are mad at yourself for not sharing with your father about how you felt a long time ago. Breathe. It's not them. Let it go.

I let out one big sigh and said, "I am so sorry for my tone and my language. I am just lost right now," I said, putting my hand over my mouth and crying.

Vanessa and my grandmother put their hands over my shoulders. "It's okay, Taneshia," Vanessa said.

We saw my dad moving and grunting, hoping that maybe all the commotion woke him up. "Jay, Jay … are you up? Taneshia is here, Jay," my grandmother said while rubbing my dad's legs.

I softly ran my fingers through my dad's hair. His beard was fully grown, and his nails were long. I could tell he had been in this state for a while. "Since the last stroke, has he been up at all?"

"He was alert for about two days, and he has been in this mode for about three," Vanessa said. "I wish you would have come over the weekend. He was gripping our hands and trying to talk and everything."

I just looked at her. I wanted to say something, but it wasn't worth it. I refused to be popping off on people the rest of the time I was there. I was there to see my dad and be with him, and that's what I was going to do.

My cousin rubbed me on the shoulder and gestured that we step out for a while. I was thankful she had broken up some of the tension and was taking me away for a moment.

As we sat in the cafeteria, eating salad and chips, we were approached by a doctor who shared that, based on my dad's age and other health complications, he was unsure if he could survive two strokes. My cousin asked questions, but I just sat there, sad and angry, with tears streaming down my face. I knew the reality was that he might be passing away, but I didn't want to admit it. I was still in disbelief that only six months had gone by. Everything felt so hard and long. Life felt like a nightmare that I couldn't wake up from.

I was almost drowning in my tears. They just kept pouring from my eyes, and I didn't know what to do. I held my cousin's hand. She placed her shoulder against mine and whispered in my ear, "I think you should say what you wanna say now, Taneshia. I keep praying, but I don't know if he is gonna make it. The pastor is coming tomorrow."

I wished I would've come earlier. I told myself I was coming when he was released from the hospital because that would've been when he needed me. But I wondered if I hadn't rushed to my dad because, my whole life, I didn't feel like he had ever rushed for me.

As a young child, I went through a lot. I walked home by

myself from school, got picked on by bullies, was diagnosed with diabetes at the age of sixteen, and spent two days in ICU with numerous tubes in my body. And my dad wasn't there for any of it. My mind went back to how sad I felt in the hospital, crying out to God, with neither of my parents present. My mom was working, visiting me between breaks and before she went to her second job. My dad didn't call or anything. In his defense, perhaps my mom didn't tell him I was in the hospital. I couldn't remember every detail, but what I do remember is feeling abandoned and alone. Was that the real reason I hadn't rushed to be there? Maybe this was my punishment. Because I was in my feelings and bitter, I was forced to watch my father pass away.

I looked at my cousin, shocked. "Pastor?" I said. "For what? Does everyone think he is dying?"

"No, but we have to prepare, Taneshia. We don't know what's gonna happen. Two strokes in one month is not good on anyone, especially with your dad being seventy-two. We just have to pray. Come on, let's go back upstairs," she said, patting me on my thigh.

I tossed the rest of my salad in the garbage, and we walked to the elevator, headed back to my dad's room to find him in the same condition. I found a chair in the corner and held his hand. My grandmother was knitting, and Vanessa was watching television.

I looked at my grandmother, stood, and gave her a hug. I softly whispered in her ear, "Sorry, Grandma."

"It's okay, honey. This is hard for all of us. I've got thick skin. If you would have upset me, I would have let you know. Taneshia, you have to stop telling yourself that you're the 'other daughter.' You are the second daughter, the baby. You feed yourself information that isn't true, and it is hurting you."

I listened to her with love and hope. I had never heard anything so beautiful from her before. I wondered if she was right. Perhaps it was all me. It wouldn't be the first time my mind made me feel like I was crazy.

"I agree. Taneshia, your dad loves you. You came when you could. I was just saying that he was more alert last week. I didn't mean it as if you should have come then. The tickets were expensive. You came when you could. The thing is, you are here," Vanessa said.

"Yeah, that's true," I said, but I didn't believe it. *Does he really know I'm here? Did I come when I could? Maybe I should have run up one of my credit cards?*

I honestly didn't realize how serious things were. I had no idea he wasn't responsive or alert. I would have come earlier. I couldn't continue to beat myself up. I had to sit in the feeling of knowing my dad might be passing away, and if he was, figure out how I wanted to spend the last moments with him and what I wanted to say.

All the pieces of my life were starting to come together. I was realizing that this rainbow of peace and love I thought would be my "healing" didn't look beautiful at all. Healing from codependency and people pleasing looks lonely, hard, strange, and foreign. Second-guessing myself and wondering if I've made the right decisions were parts of healing. The first five years were just repetition and busy work, trying to understand the fundamentals of what it means to live my own life and not take care of others. Now, I was actually taking the test of living life, and it felt like I was failing at a drastic rate. I was making mental plans about what I would do if he left me.

As memories from our previous trip that year floated in and

out of my mind, I could see how negative self-talk played a major role. My core belief was that my dad didn't want me; no one wanted me. That I was lucky my mother even had me because I was a burden. That core belief was ignited by comments I'd heard growing up, like what my dad had said: "My life was okay, and then I had you." Sometimes, from frustration, my mother would say, "I work two jobs for you." I didn't understand what any of those statements meant at the age of eight or nine, and neither one of my parents knew how to explain or even felt it needed to be explained. Subsequently, I ended up believing I was lucky to even have people who loved me because I was unlovable. That core belief had been leading my entire life, not just the relationship with my dad, but with everyone. It ultimately led me to become codependent and use pleasing people as a coping mechanism to connect with them because I thought showing up as myself wasn't enough.

People who struggle with codependency often believe that by doing what others want them to do, they will be okay. They spend their entire life running from their feelings of rejection and abandonment, only to be rejected and abandoned anyway due to the type of people they get into friendships and intimate relationships with. I could see how I had connected with people based on low self-worth. Because Joanne thought I was funny, easy going, and a problem solver, she became friends with me. I, in turn, made sure I listened to all her problems and helped her solve each one to show my own worth in the relationship. Now that I was trying to be friends with her based on who I really was and not what I could do for her, she was confused. She expected me to be that version of myself who supported her and helped her because that was who she had been friends with for ten years. I had changed the script, and she struggled with that.

In addition to that, I could see how my assumption that I was going to be rejected by my father and family caused me to automatically behave a certain way around them. I thought back to how I felt in my grandma's home. There I was, a thirty-five-year-old woman, acting like I was eight years old, tip-toeing around the house, wanting to share my feelings with her but afraid she wouldn't care. I should have just walked into her room, laid on her bed, and treated her like she really is my grandmother. I was waiting for a response from her, a cue from her, that she had no idea I needed.

That's the problem with being codependent. Most of the time, we don't know it's okay to have needs, and we don't know what we need. We expect others to help us figure it out, which is almost impossible because we don't communicate with them. It's a cycle we're stuck in until we get the strength to move past our fear and find ways to communicate our needs.

I shook my head in disbelief that all these epiphanies were coming during this stage of my life. I had wasted a lot of years assuming people didn't love me, only to realize that everybody loved me. They just didn't understand what I needed to feel loved.

I held my father's hand, looking at the shapes and grooves in his fingers, seeing how they were the same as mine. *I have my dad's hands.* I rubbed each finger, wishing he would wake up. Occasionally, my dad made grunting sounds and turned toward me, but he didn't wake up. We all sat there for about four hours, in shock that the man we all loved seemed to be leaving us.

He Knows My Name

had been in Tampa for three days, and it was time to return home. My dad's condition remained the same, and we were all at a loss for words about what was happening. Vanessa and I arrived at the hospital early that morning so I could spend all day with him. The hospital was preparing for my dad to be transported to a nursing home. Vanessa needed support for choosing the best facility and getting him there properly, and I was happy to be there to help.

As she and I neared dad's room, one of the nurses approached her. "Oh, Taneshia, I have to talk with her. Go ahead and go in," Vanessa said.

"Okay," I said softly. I took it as God's way of finally giving me alone time with my dad. There were always so many of us in the room every day, and I didn't feel comfortable asking everyone to leave.

I walked into my dad's room to find the doctor there, checking charts and writing things down. I hadn't seen him since I had been there. He was a brown-skinned African American male with a fade and goatee. *Oh, thank God. The doctor is here. Maybe I can get some answers.*

"Hi. How are you? I'm Taneshia Johnson, Mr. Johnson's daughter."

"No introduction needed. You look just like your dad." We both laughed.

"Yeah, everybody says that. Thank you. I am happy you're here. I'm leaving tomorrow, and I really want to know what's next for my dad. He has been unresponsive for the last three days, and today, I hear he is going to a nursing home. Why?"

The doctor took a deep breath. "Yeah, well, may I show you some charts?"

"Yes, I'd love to see."

He pulled out two graphs and pointed to various parts of the brain. I recognized some parts from what I had learned in school, but I didn't know what everything meant. "So, if you take a look here, you can see that the left side of your dad's brain had a small amount of damage, which mostly controls movement in his legs and shoulders, but it wasn't bad. However, after the second stroke, we see how the right side *really* had a big impact." The doctor noticed the tears coming down my face. "Oh, I am so sorry. I didn't know you were crying. Is this too much?"

I shook my head while wiping tears with my t-shirt. "No, no, I need to know. So this part that looks like a whirlwind around my dad's head … Is this a stroke?"

"Yes, this scan lets us know what parts are impacted."

"Well, I mean, the whole side is in a whirlwind, so the whole side is affected, right?"

The doctor took another deep breath, and with endearing eyes, he responded. "Yes, Ms. Johnson."

I became overwhelmed with grief. I started shaking and stumbling over my words. "So really, my dad is not coming back from this. He will be like this forever?" I said with a face full of tears.

The doctor looked around and then looked at my dad. "It's very likely that Mr. Johnson will not recover."

I ran to the side of the bed and held my dad's hand, placing it on my face and crying. I recalled every memory with him from childhood to now. Seeing my dad's smiling face as he picked me up from the airport, him asking me what I wanted to do for the summer, and just enjoying my time with him overall. I wondered how I could've ever denied his love for me. I was growing to understand that because I wasn't healed, I had been viewing my relationship with my father from a part of me that was hurt, rejected, and felt unloved. I couldn't see past what I thought my reality was. Only recently had I grown up emotionally to be the thirty-five-year-old woman who was standing next to him. Before, every summer, I had been showing up as that six-year-old who wanted her daddy to love and care for her and protect her from the world. I cried over him, feeling stupid and ashamed of myself for our last face-to-face encounter. I was happy I'd told him how I felt and stood up for myself, but sad about the way I'd chosen to do it. Beating myself up wouldn't bring my father back, but I couldn't help but cry, not only because he was possibly dying, but because I never got a chance to say that I understood how hard it must have been for him trying to coparent from thousands of miles away. And even though I didn't understand his absence at times, I forgave him.

The doctor quietly walked out, leaving just my dad and me. I rubbed his head while watching my tears land on the bed. I held his hand, and he gripped my fingers. I wondered if he was alert.

I decided to take a chance and talk to him, possibly for the last time. "Dad, it's Taneshia. Lord Jesus, I am so scared. I wish you would wake up, Daddy. I want you to know I love you, and it's okay. Can you hear me?" I took a breath to pause and wipe my nose. "Dad, I love the time we had together. Thank you for what you did. I even thank you for what you didn't do and what you didn't know to do. I have been expecting you to give me the guidance, love, and support I needed, but really, I see you have done what you can. It's up to me now. I'm sorry that I was expecting you to give me something you didn't know I needed. Thank you for doing what you can. These last six months have been amazing. Our talks have been so helpful. I wish I would have told you what I needed a long time ago. You were always open to it, weren't you?" I said with a smile. I gave him a kiss on the forehead.

The doctor returned with Vanessa, who was in tears. I assumed he must have told her the same news he'd told me.

"Mrs. Johnson, we are getting ready to transport Mr. Johnson to the nursing home. Let me give you the address for you and your daughter," we heard a nurse say from the hallway.

Another nurse came in and changed my dad's clothes, grooming him to leave, then she checked his vitals one last time. Two more nurses came in to help lift my dad and place him on a different bed for the transport to the car.

As they lifted him, his eyes opened! I yelled out to him, "Dad, Dad, it's Taneshia, Dad!"

My dad looked at me, seemingly confused, but he couldn't speak.

"Daddy, its me," I said, crying and holding his hand. "Do you see me, Daddy?"

"He does, sweetie," Vanessa said, rubbing my shoulder. "Jay, Taneshia is here."

My dad was still looking at me, and I saw a small smile emerge on his face. It remained until he fell back into the coma.

"Come on, sweetie. Let's get in the car, so we can meet them there," Vanessa said.

I wiped my tears "Okay."

We followed the transport car to the nursing home. As we pulled up to the building, we couldn't help but notice how small it was. I got out of the car and went to Vanessa's side to help her.

"This place looks like a dump, huh?" she said. "I may have to move him from here. The other places aren't covered by his insurance, though. You know your dad was always bargaining, even down to the health insurance he chose."

"Yeah, Dad is crazy." We smiled as we walked to the door.

An African American young woman spoke to us through a glass door. She glanced back and forth between Vanessa and me, and asked, "Can I help you, ma'am?"

Vanessa looked at me, seemingly confused and shocked because the woman was talking to us through the glass. "Hi, my name is Vanessa Johnson. My husband was just transported here from the hospital. I want to talk to someone about his stay and also make sure he has what he needs for the night."

The girl seemed to be confused about what to say. "Okay, um, ma'am, visiting hours have ended, but since he just got here, let me see what we can do.

She left and returned with another woman who wore a badge and stated that she was a registered nurse. They both smiled at us while opening the door.

As we walked to my dad's room, every horror story I'd heard about nursing homes came to mind. The walls were light pink, and the carpet was dark green. The rails were an off-white color, and they'd obviously been painted over several times. The whole building gave me a nasty vibe. It smelled of Clorox and Lysol. Some of the patients were sitting in the hallway in front of their rooms, looking at Vanessa and me as we walked by. With every step, I feared what my dad's room would look like. I hated that he was here, but there was nothing I could do. I didn't have any money to pay for another facility, and I still had a small amount of hope that maybe he would wake up again like he had earlier, and he could leave this place.

We got to my dad's room and saw he had the space to himself. It had the same light pink walls but with linoleum floors. The room was clean. There was a bathroom and sink along with a small closet. My dad had all the machines hooked up to him, except the one that gave him food. As soon as I noticed it, I immediately spoke up to the nurse. "Where is the machine that gives him food; it's not here," I said frantically. I glanced at Vanessa, who was now also concerned that it wasn't there.

"Yeah, that one has to be particularly placed inside of your dad's stomach; we don't have a technician here tonight who can do it the way it needs to be done, but I promise you it will be done tomorrow.

"Tomorrow, I'm leaving!" I screeched.

"It's okay, Taneshia. I will make sure they do it," Vanessa said while holding my hand.

"Okay," I said, trying to calm down. I sat in the chair next to my dad, examining his face and holding his hands.

"I will give you guys some time. Since visiting hours are over, just stay as long as you'd like," the nurse whispered.

Vanessa and I smiled with gratitude. "Thank you," we both said.

Vanessa went to the other side of my dad's bed. "Jay, you gotta wake up, Jay. Taneshia is leaving tomorrow."

I remembered some of my dad's favorite songs and suddenly got an idea. "Hey, I wonder if we should try music! Maybe that will wake him up." Vanessa agreed, and I pulled my phone out of my purse and opened the music app. "Maybe I should play Kirk Franklin's new album. I know he likes that one." I was so excited to have thought of an idea.

"Yes, he does. Any song is good. Your dad loves him."

I played a song called "God Like You." It was one of my favorites from the album too, and it would get anyone up and moving and praising God. Vanessa and I sang the words, and we noticed his eyes twitching as if he was trying to open them. His feet were also moving side to side. Vanessa moved his arm back and forth. I took the other arm and did the same, as if we were trying to get him to dance in his bed. We both smiled, noticing that he started moving on his own.

Just as soon as our happiness came, we noticed that my dad's feet stopped moving as much and his head tilted toward my side. The song ended and another song by Kirk Franklin called "My World Needs You" began playing. It was a slower song. I wasn't sure if my dad had stopped moving because of the change of song or if he was going back into his coma. Before I knew it, my tears started again.

"Daddy, please wake up, Daddy. Please wake up," I pleaded.

Vanessa and I both looked up to see that my dad had opened his eyes. "Taneshia! Look! Jay, can you hear us?"

"Dad! It's me, Taneshia. I'm here." We both cried out repeatedly, trying to get him to stay with us.

My dad looked at me as if he saw me, although I wasn't sure. I felt a light grip on my hand, and I smiled at him with tears falling from my chin to his blanket. He gave me another gaze before drifting off. His eyes slowly rolled up to the sky as if he were being taken somewhere else, someplace where we couldn't go, and then they closed. I put my empty hand over my mouth and cried inside of it. I looked at Vanessa to see her also crying. We were both so hopeful that he was slowly coming back to us. We wiped our tears, allowing the music to continue to play, hoping he would wake up again. We sat there for almost two hours. I prayed, cried, and prayed some more, but my dad never woke up again.

Vanessa and I got back from the nursing home late. I decided to pack my bag as soon as we returned, so I could sleep in a little before my flight in the morning. During the ride home, we were silent, and when we arrived, all we could do was look at each other, give each other a big hug and kiss, and go to our rooms. We were scared and didn't know what to say to each other.

The morning had come, and it was time for me to return home. Even though I was sad about leaving, I knew I had to. I got my bag together and placed it in the car. I went to see if Vanessa was awake, and surprisingly found her sitting on the bed. "Hey," she said, smiling and wiping her eyes.

"Hey." I sat beside her and held her hand. "I wish I didn't have to leave," I said softly.

"Me too," she said with a faint smile. Her eyes were red, and several tissues lay on the bed next to her. I didn't know how long she had been crying, but I was sad that she was.

"So, what's the next step for him?" I didn't want to bring it up, but I wanted to know before I left.

"Well, he is breathing well on his own, and outside of bed sores, he is pretty stable. I put in a request for him to be turned and bathed more. They are going to replace the feeding tube today. So we just have to wait and see if your dad comes out of this."

"I believe he will. God knows. I will continue to pray. It will be okay."

"You think so?" she asked, looking at me with a small beam of hope in her eyes.

"Yeah, he will. God knows we just started building a relationship I am proud of. Reading together, longer calls; it really has been great," I said, smiling.

"I know," Vanessa said, getting excited. "Your dad shared too. Y'all were reading books and talking about your dating life and everything. He said you were writing a book too."

"Yeah, I am. I sent my manuscript to the editor before you called me."

"That's great, Taneshia. I know your dad will be the first to read it," Vanessa said, holding my hand with both of hers.

"Yeah, I'm sure he will be," I said with my head down in doubt. I didn't know what to believe. One thing I know about God is, although He loves us and understands our emotions, His will comes before all things. And like the rest of my life this year, I didn't know what God's will was going to look like. "Well, I better try to make it out of here, or else I will be here another few days, searching for another flight," I said, getting up from the bed.

I looked down at my hand to find that Vanessa was gripping it a little stronger. Those same red eyes were now spilling a cascade of tears. She cried quietly to herself. I stood there for a few seconds, trying to find the right words to say. *Just say everything will be okay, but will it? What if it's not? Now, you have given her pipe dreams. I have to say something. I can't just leave her here in this state. Regardless of everything, she did somewhat support your childhood. Maybe even the money your dad was sending was partially hers; you don't know. You should say something.*

After wrestling with these thoughts, I finally said, "Vanessa, I am so sorry. However things work out, it will work out for the good. At least that's what I'm telling myself. I have to. It's all I have." I sat back down on the bed and gave her a big hug, then walked out.

I took one last glance over the guest bedroom I'd slept in and the living room to make sure I had everything, then I walked out to the car. I got in, and every tear I was trying to hold in to be strong for Vanessa came out. I strapped my seatbelt on and cried. I couldn't believe I was even going through this. This year had taken my mind and heart by storm, and I felt like a wreck. Dr. Karen's words kept going through my mind. *"This is what healing looks like … This is what healing looks like …"* I still couldn't believe she was right. All the work I had done to express how I feel to people, advocate my own needs, and center myself had paid off. But the idea of my parents not being around anymore never came to mind. I thought my years of being upset and disappointed by my dad had ended with us loving each other. Now, all my hopes and dreams of my dad holding my first child or walking me down the aisle were fading away. I didn't know how to feel.

I picked up my phone, trying to figure out who I could reach out to for support. Who could hold space for me right then? I knew Ashton would, but it wouldn't be sincere. It would be just another tactic he would use later to make me feel guilty for setting boundaries with him. In addition to that, I had learned a long time ago with Shawn that going back to the person who hurt you can never be a place of healing. Joanne was possibly an option. Even though we had a rough ending to our last conversation, she was still my friend. Deep down in my heart I knew she loved me, and I knew that when I told her what was happening with my dad, she would stop what she was doing to be there for me. I went back and forth in my head for a long time, and then decided to step out and text her, to stop assuming what would happen and just ask for the help and support I needed.

I grabbed my phone, clicked on her contact, and texted her: Hey, Joanne. I am not sure where we stand. I know our last conversation was heavy. Just wanted to share that my dad had a stroke and now he has had another one. I am really scared. Leaving Tampa now. It would be great to hear from you. Bye.

I started the car and pulled out of the driveway. I turned on Pandora and connected it to my Bluetooth. The first song to play was my favorite track by Tasha Cobbs "He Knows My Name." As I turned each right and left turn, leading to the freeway, I reminisced on driving with my dad and hearing this song. Every tree, every corner, every Waffle House I passed reminded me of him. I remembered being there just about six months ago, and things were good. I regretted every minute I'd spent in my feelings about not getting the love I wanted.

So many popped off in my mind; it was like the Fourth of July in my head. I was putting everything together and coming to the realization that it was me. My thoughts had been in the way of me getting the love I deserved from family and friends.

Even though I was emotionally drained from setting boundaries and expressing myself, I was getting the results I wanted and needed. Ashton was finally gone. The madness of thinking I was delusional for wanting more but never getting what I needed from him was gone. All the kissing and spending time together was confusing. I was settling for a person who never had any plans to commit. He was using me for emotional support, and I couldn't even see it. It had felt so good to be loved and seen that I allowed those feelings to get in the way of what I really wanted, which was a relationship and a commitment from a man who loved me and loved God.

I even reflected on my friendship with Joanne. Maybe she was just loving me the way she knew how. Did I really have to cut her off? Maybe I just needed to find a group of people that could pour into me in every season of my life—bad, good, ugly, and insane. Joanne could still be a friend, but maybe not worthy of the label "best friend," and maybe she never was. Maybe no one was. Maybe I was supposed to be my own best friend. The only person who had been carrying me through this journey was me ... and God. I only told friends and family the aftermath.

I don't know how I managed to do it, but I got to the airport. I saw the rental car signs and made a left toward the exit. I drove down the ramp, remembering, this time, that it would be a winding road, strengthening my grip on the wheel.

I took my luggage out of the trunk and walked toward the

entrance to check in. My phone rang. It was Joanne. "Hey, girl," I said.

"Taneshia! What the hell, girl! Your dad had a stroke? When? Why didn't you call me? Oh, my God. I am so sorry. I really had no idea what you were going through earlier this year. You just saw him, bitch!"

Wow! It has been a while since I've talked to her. I forgot she goes a hundred miles a minute. But I know it's all love. "Yeah, girl. It's been a journey. I'm at the airport right now, going home."

"Home? Why? You should just stay there."

"I wish I could, girl, but I've been here four days already. My dad hasn't really woken up since I've been here. I just watch him day in and day out, slowly float away, girl. It's sad."

"I'm so sorry, Taneshia. I didn't realize you had been there that long already."

"Yeah, girl. He had the first stroke a few weeks ago and was recovering well. But then, he had this one, and it's just been crazy. I think the thing that gets me the most is I don't even know if he knows I'm here." My face grew warm, and I started crying. I couldn't stop walking because I only had about forty-five minutes left before my flight. I had to keep going, talking and crying, watching people look at me like I was crazy. "Here I go again. I'm just waterfalls all the damn time. Sorry, girl. Anyway, what's new with you? It's been a while," I said, trying to remember that all conversations weren't about me.

"Taneshia, stop it. Your dad is sick. Honestly, girl, it sounds like he is dying. What are you gonna do?"

I found a bench close to my gate and sat down. I took a deep breath. "I don't know, sis." I cried. "Girl, I just want my life to fast-forward to a day when things will be better."

"I know, girl. Just let it out."

I allowed myself to cry freely. After a few minutes, I wiped my tears and started running toward my gate. "Girl, oh Lord! The flight leaves in like twenty-five minutes. You know they're already boarding!"

"Did yo' ass check in late? You with Southwest? You know you're gonna be in seat C99 by now!"

"You know I did," I said, laughing.

"Hopefully, you get an aisle seat with that weak-ass bladder you got!"

"Aw, you cold, Jo!"

"Nah, but seriously, I heard what you said during our last conversation, and you were right. I was trippin'. You have always been the "strong friend," and I guess seeing you break down just made me scared. Who else I'mma call with all this shit?" We chuckled. "But I started going back to codependency meetings, and I told a girl at the meeting what happened, and she got me all the way together. I want you to know I heard your boundaries, Taneshia, even though you didn't fully state them at first. I heard them the second time. My drama is too much right now, and you are in a season of needing me, not the other way around."

Listen to my friend. Did she just earn the "best friend" title back. Let's see how things go first, but I think she got it back. "Okay, Ms. Joanne, listen to you! May I just change one thing you said? It is not that your life is too much, nor is it too much drama. We've both got drama. I just need you now. It will go back to you needing me. That's the healthy flow of friendship; it ebbs and flows like a river, so we both get filled up."

"Listen to you, Ms. TJ! Okay, girl! My friend is a whole author and shit now, poppin' her wisdom!" Joanne said jokingly.

"You know I have learned a little something, something. You know I'm healing and growing. Got a new therapist now and stuff. Yeah, yo' girl is poppin' now."

"My girl!" We shared another giggle.

"Listen, catch that damn flight, 'cause I know how late you roll, Taneshia. I love you, and please call me about your dad. Don't suffer alone, okay?"

"Okay … Joanne?" I said softly.

"Yeah?"

"I love you."

I heard silence on the other end and then sobbing. "I never thought I would hear those words again from you. And it scared me so much. I love you too, you codependent heffa."

"I love your codependent, people-pleasing ass too." We hung up. I smiled at the phone screen before placing it in my purse, happy to have my friend again.

I got on the flight and headed home. During the entire six-hour flight, I did nothing but think of my dad and cry. I remembered when I was six years old; I would get excited about coming back home each summer. Thinking about returning to my mom and eating snacks on the plane always made me quickly pack my bags and smile while doing it. As I got older, that feeling never changed. I was always uncomfortable when visiting my dad in Tampa. I loved my dad and that side of the family, but my thoughts always made me feel uneasy. I would always wonder whether they loved me or not, and if they did, why I didn't really know them or have a relationship with them. The thoughts haunted me all summer until it was time to go home. This ride home felt different. It felt like I had wasted years questioning if my dad and his side of the family loved me, only to find that they did. All it took was me stepping out of the beliefs I had about myself and communicating my needs.

Up until I was six years old, my entire life had involved only my mom and great aunt. It felt different being with my dad, but I ended up having great summers. My dad was an entrepreneur. He had his own business cleaning windows. He even had a contract with the United States Postal Service when he was still in Alabama and earned a consistent income, with employees and everything. I would help too. My dad used to give me fifty dollars for a week's pay. It may not seem like much, but at twelve years old, I felt rich. Most times, I would only wipe the mirrors; his employees did the hard work.

Most summers were like that until I was about seventeen, and then I started working during the summers to make money. Our relationship shifted a little because my dad also had an accident when I was fifteen, so we lost touch for a couple of years. But for my high school graduation, he and Vanessa came, and in college, he started calling me twice a week and continued to call me regularly from then on. We would only talk for five to ten minutes. I interpreted that as him not wanting to know what was going on with me. I could now clearly see that's not what it was. He wasn't a talker, and he didn't know that I was. I couldn't wrap my head around the fact that the man I saw lying in the nursing home, fighting to look at me was the same man from my memories.

We landed back in California, and I was on my way to baggage claim. I called everyone in my family to let them know I had landed safely: Vanessa, my sister, my grandmother, and my aunt. I didn't get a chance to make it to Waffle House before I left. I wanted to go to the one my dad and I had gone to earlier that year.

I tried to think of ways I could pick myself up and believe that, even though the doctors said one thing, God had the final say.

After waiting forever for my luggage, it finally came. I heard my phone vibrating. It was a text message from my editor: Hi, Taneshia. Love the concept you have in this first draft. I have sent it back to you. After we have our virtual meeting, you have thirty days to review. I am excited to support you for your first book.

I immediately started dancing! I couldn't believe it. I had actually written a whole-ass book! I had an editor! For my whole life, I thought social work was it for me. I never even thought I could write a book. This was a moment I wanted to share with my mom and dad, but my mom was the only parent I could reach out to. I decided to wait until I got home to share the news with her and enjoy the bliss of completing a book.

I took chances that whole year. I was learning that in order to heal from codependency, I had to define who I was. The process was hard, but it was needed. So much of my life had been focused on other people and what they needed; I had never taken a moment to reflect on who I was. I allowed the roles I played for other people to define me and consequently lead me to a road of depression. Everything was making sense for once. That was the reason I wanted to title my book *When Depression and Anxiety Have a Voice*, because I finally had a voice. I had released myself from the invisible shackles on my ankles, and I was finally able to walk my own path.

I didn't realize the path involved losing friends, hating my job, meeting a narcissist, and wondering what I was doing with my life, but it did. I had to stop judging myself or wishing my life was someone else's and just *live*, learning how to trust me and the decisions I made for my own life. Knowing that if I set a boundary with someone and that person decided they no longer wanted to deal with me because of it, it was okay. Because if a person couldn't respect my boundaries then they'd always cause issues in my life. I was learning to accept that I was evolving and growing, and things couldn't stay the same. One thing I did want to stay the same, though, was my dad being around to see it. I didn't know how to handle the thought of him being gone.

Just as I was going down memory lane, I heard my phone ring. It was Joanne. "Hey, sis!" I said, answering the phone.

"Hey, girl. How are you? Are you on your way home?"

"Yes. I don't know why I deal with this damn BART train, girl. I should have just caught an Uber or drove," I said, shaking my head while walking to the train.

"Well, I would have picked you up. You always do things alone, Taneshia. Folks gotta beg you to help you. That shit is crazy; I hope you know that."

"Well, birds of a feather flock together; you do the exact same crap," I said, smiling.

"Shut up, girl." We both chuckled.

"Do you wanna come pick me up? 'Cause I will definitely sit my happy self down at this airport and wait."

"Say less, ho. I'm down the street. What terminal are you at?"

"I'm at the red one," I said.

There was a pause then a burst of laughter. "Sis, they're all red. You're at Southwest, right?"

"You know I'm kinda slow, girl. Yes, Southwest."

"You love you some Southwest."

I eventually heard cars and horns in the background and started looking for Joanne's car. I soon saw her car about two blocks down and walked toward her, waving.

Joanne pulled over to the curb. She got out and ran to me. I never understood why she wanted to be my friend. My low self-esteem told me she was my friend only because I gave her advice, listened to her, and helped her figure out her life. But this new version of myself was trying to understand that people did genuinely love me. It wasn't because of what I did for them; it was because of who I am.

"Taneshia! OMG, sis, I missed you!" she screeched with open arms.

We gave each other a big hug. She had tears in her eyes and so did I. I grabbed her hand. "I am so happy to see you."

My smile soon faded when I noticed that Joanne had bruises all over her knuckles. I looked at her face; the side of it was battered with cut marks and what looked like bruises from a fist. "Jo, what the hell is this?" I said, pushing her hair out of her face to get a closer look.

"Girl, just get in the car." Joanne said, while putting my bag in the trunk and running to the driver side of the car.

The light turned green, and Joanne stepped on the gas, navigating the turns of a descending hill. "Yeah, it's been a lot, girl. I don't even know where to start or if I should start because you are going through a lot too." Joanne wiped tears from her eyes with her bruised hand.

I was silent for a few minutes, reflecting on our conversation when I was in Los Angeles and when I was in Florida visiting my dad. I looked out the passenger window, wondering if this was yet another relationship I had been viewing all wrong. *What the hell? How long has Jo been going through this? Have you been so focused on you that you forgot about her? Wait ... but I should be thinking about me, right?*

"Taneshia, I know you. Get out of your head," Joanne said, holding my hand. "It's okay, girl. How could you have known? I never said anything. I really didn't know how to bring it up. And I think every time you brought up your real emotions, I was envious and jealous because I was trying to figure out why I couldn't express mine. Why couldn't I really tell you what was going on? Yes, I was embarrassed, but I have been embarrassed many of day with you. Sleeping with a lot of guys and going on fancy trips is one thing, but telling somebody I am allowing a man to beat me up? I didn't know how to say that, sis."

I just looked at her in awe of her transparency and what she was saying. Eventually, I was able to get out of my head and open my mouth. "How long has this been going on?"

Joanne laughed. "Girl, the whole damn relationship. The first three months were great. I mean he was like my dream guy. And then out of nowhere, he threw me against the car one day when we were leaving a restaurant. He told me the dress I had on was too short and every man was looking at my butt. He accused me of trying to lure other guys to me because I wasn't happy with him."

"What?" I said in shock.

"Right! Stupid! Before I knew it, girl, I became a statistic out here. We have really amazing sex; he cooks for me, rubs my feet, and tells me how much he loves me. And then as soon as I do something he doesn't like ... whap! Right up my face. I got this bruise from him pushing me in the shower," she said, pointing to the mark on her face.

"The shower! What the hell!"

Joanne shook her head, "Girl, the man was literally making love to me, kissing me on the mouth, and because I wouldn't let him pull my hair, he took my head and slammed my face against the glass. Needless to say, I left the other day. I'm back with my mom. He has been calling me eight to ten times a day. I just ignore the calls. My mom says I should get a restraining order." Joanne was crying.

"I agree with her. This is bullshit! I can't believe this, girl!" I said, wiping tears from my eyes, still in a state of shock from hearing what was really going on with my friend.

I looked out the window again, thinking about my friend and my life. It looked like both Joanne and I had run into narcissistic men. I was grateful that Ashton wasn't physically abusive. The psychological games he played and the emotional abuse alone were too much for me. I couldn't imagine if he was also hitting me.

This whole healing journey is about, not only holding space for ourselves, but also those we are in relationships with—friends, family members, coworkers, partners, etc. Everyone is just living life, trying to figure things out. We are all experts of our own lives, but we can't expect people to read our minds and know what we need. It is up to us to speak up and express our needs without shame or guilt and be ready to hear the other person's point of view. We must be active listeners, finding balance between when it's time to share and when it's time to be present for others. And when we get confused and become unsure, that's when we need to have transparent conversations with those we love to identify who needs who in the relationship. And then figure out how we can both feel supported, so we're not left feeling depleted by each other's life issues.

I regretted cutting Joanne off. I could see she really did need me. And now that we both were being honest with each other, we could properly support each other. It took Joanne and I getting individual help from others to be able to support each other how we both needed. I needed a listening ear while I was in Florida, and she needed me now.

We must learn to read our loved ones' cues and point out behavior that is abnormal to them, no longer assessing what we think they need, but giving them an opportunity to tell us. In return, we will find that the other person will begin to carry their own weight in the relationship, preventing us from feeling like things are one-sided.

This was the new rule I had to carry in my own relationships, starting with Joanne. Joanne and I were individually healing and finally able to support each other from a healthy space. She and I thought being best friends meant we had to be "ride or die" with each other and be each other's personal diary, but we were only sharing our trauma stories back and forth with no real solutions. I wanted her to hear me, and she wanted me to hear her, but neither one of us was ready to hear the truth until now. I had hope for Joanne and me again, and it felt good because I really needed her now. And I could tell she needed me too.

Despite crazy traffic, Joanne and I made it to my apartment in one piece. She pointed to my car in the carport and said, "You see that car right there? Next time you travel to the airport, you need to take her too. Sis is over here lonely. All the other cars gone and shit."

"Joanne, you stupid!" I said, getting out of the car. We laughed together. "Full transparency, I want to be there for you. I know I am going through it. But let me be the one to say I need a break. Don't isolate yourself, girl. I am glad you went back to the codependency meetings. You need a community to keep you strong. Domestic abuse is real, and it can be addictive. You need people to help you in hard times, so you won't go back to him."

Joanne and I were holding hands. "You're right, Taneshia, I do. Parts of me feel crazy for leaving. He took care of me. Girl, I didn't have to do nothing. But it's not worth this."

"Girl, it's not worth your life or your pretty-ass face. Speaking of your face, I see you've been getting facials without me again." I said, while pulling Joanne's hair to the side.

"Ho, we weren't talking. I didn't even know if we were still friends. I have to stay cute so I can get some new friends … before they find out I'm crazy."

Joanne lifted my suitcase from her car and rolled it over to me. We gave each other a kiss on the cheek and a hug. "Bye, Jo!"

"Bye T. Love you. And keep me posted about your dad, *please!*"

"I will."

I went upstairs to find my mom asleep. I really wanted to tell her about my book and updates about Dad, but I didn't want to wake her. I went to my room, turned on some soft jazz music, and started unpacking my clothes. As I unpacked, I thought more about Joanne, my job, my dad, and me. Life was funny. I was convinced that things were supposed to work out differently now that I was focused on me. This whole emotional self-care thing was looking like a living nightmare for me. Having to make scary decisions every day, questioning everything I did, and learning who I was all in one process … If this was healing, I was convinced I was becoming a master at it. I took the ups with the downs, was learning to speak up for myself with everyone, regardless of who they were, and I was stepping out and doing something I had always wanted to do—write a book.

Even though things were rocky, I smiled as I reflected because I remembered just a few years ago when I was struggling, processing my feelings of depression and pleasing people and learning how to get back to me. I see now that it never was about getting back to me; it was about learning the new woman I was becoming and embracing her.

I chuckled to myself. *Damn, Taneshia, you really got a whole new therapist, said hell no to a job that paid more money, got rid of Ashton's narcissistic ass and you told your dad your true feelings.* I was in awe of myself.

"I guess this is really what it is all about," I said aloud.

A few days passed, and I was getting resettled. I had another therapy session with Karen in a couple of days, and my appointment with my editor was coming up, and I was super excited about that. I was learning to love my new boundaries and view on life.

I got up and made my bed. I glanced at my closet, trying to figure out what to wear. I saw a cute jean dress I liked that I hadn't worn in a while. I pulled it out and headed to the shower. I stepped in and filled my loofa with a lavender liquid soap, washing my body and staring at the ceiling. Everyone that was supposed to be in my life was still here. Setting boundaries scared me because I thought that as soon as I did it, everyone would leave me and I would be alone. My mind told me I had to continue to find a way to support people or else I was no good as a person and didn't deserve to be part of their lives. That was such crap! I am beautiful, loving, and deserving of respect and love. Boundaries are designed to keep us safe. And if we don't have them, it will be more challenging for us to heal and live our lives on our terms.

It is required that you tell people how you feel and what you need. Every time you do, you will feel better about yourself. You will start to feel like you are in control of your own life. People pleasing weighs us down. We think we are in control because we are the caregivers, helping everyone else and working miracles for them. We are the "strong ones." However, in reality, everyone else is controlling us. We are shackled to their agenda, their tasks, their lives. Our inner child cries out occasionally through our anger or avoidant behavior, but we don't listen to it. We use alcohol, drugs, overworking, overeating, sex, and other "fixes" to drown it out until we lose touch with who we are and what is important to us.

I realized I had been in the shower too long and needed to get out before I was late for work. I stepped out, wrapped the towel around me, and walked back to my room. I heard the phone ringing. It was Vanessa. Even though my dad hadn't woken up yet, he was still breathing on his own, and I was praying for him and keeping my faith that he would be okay.

I decided to say a quick prayer before I answered the phone. "Dear God. Please let this be news that my dad is getting better. I love you. Amen."

"Hey, Vanessa. How are you?" I said, answering the phone.

"Taneshia, this isn't Vanessa. This is her daughter, Sandra. Taneshia, my mom is still shaken up, but I wanted to tell you that Mr. Johnson passed this morning, about an hour ago."

I collapsed on my bed and dropped the phone on the floor. I heard Sandra saying hello on the other end, but I couldn't speak.

I eventually got up, crying, desperately seeking out one of my dad's T-shirts in my closet. I found one and lay on my bed, looking out the window. I felt this day was going to come, but I didn't expect it so soon. I was thankful I had spent time with him before he passed but also felt lost and confused. I wanted to pray, but I didn't have the words. I cried, cried, and cried some more. With each tear came a memory of my dad. Seeing him smiling as I came down the escalator at the airport; his shoulders bouncing as he chuckled at my jokes; sharing a waffle with him; holding hands in the airport. It was all over.

The very thing I feared would happen had happened, and I couldn't do anything about it. I was being abandoned. My dad had left this world, and I was left here to figure things out on my own. This was a fear I'd had even in my childhood, and I just realized it as an adult. God said it was time for my dad to leave, and I had to find a way to accept it.

Healing Looks Like ...

The pain of losing a parent is one I can't explain. It's something I don't wish on anyone. And when it does happen, I pray you aren't like me—unprepared and only thinking of the things you could have done differently. My father's death made me realize why it is so important to live for myself and do things I enjoy.

I had spent my entire life caregiving for others. I was happy to have found my way, no longer allowing others to control my life or say rude things to me. Making sure everyone knows I am important and deserve respect too. And setting boundaries when needed to avoid burnout and pain. Taking care of self is what life is all about. Pouring into others and then expecting them to know when we need to be poured into is not fair to them or us. It is also unrealistic. It is a setup for disappointment and conflict in our relationships. That's what I did with my dad. I was expecting him to know what I needed and disappointed when I didn't get it. Feelings of rejection control us. Healing requires us to tap back into our needs as children and discover who we are and what is important to us.

Even under these circumstances, I was still trying my best to do that. I could tell that therapy must have been working because my entire thought process had changed. I lay there thinking about my life. Parts of me felt guilty for thinking about me and not my dad, but his death was the biggest reminder to live that I had ever gotten in my life. I knew it was my obligation to myself to have fun, do what I wanted to do, and live every day as if it were my last.

All those stories I had read and heard about the healing journey being an experience of walking into the sunset, feeling at peace and being serene came to mind. Never did I think I was going to be walking alone, crying most days, and wondering if every decision I made was the right decision. And I definitely never thought I would find peace with the loss of my dad. I thought the momentum we had built would be the foundation for our new relationship, that we would continue to tell each other how we felt, talk on the phone every other day, and have real conversations that could help me make decisions for me. But I guess God's plan was for me to do my healing work while my dad was here and understand him better, so I could, in turn, understand myself better and my needs. I was happy he was able to see me start to make necessary changes and had a front-row seat to me turning down a job I didn't want, setting boundaries with him and others, and finally living my own life.

I carry him in my spirit every day. Every time I get anxious or worry about whether I am doing something right, I remember my dad. I think back to conversations we had and decide to choose me instead of other people.

The ideas you may have had about healing like, "just learning to say no" or "not doing as much for people as you usually do" are not what the process looks like. Healing from people pleasing involves all of that *and* loving yourself enough to know you are worthy of the changes. You are worthy of asking for help. You are worthy of asking for respect. These things are not something you have to earn; they are things you should be given automatically because you are a human being and you have needs. Often, we think we have to earn love because everything we have, we had to work for. No one gave us anything, so why should love be any different? But it is. We must believe that we are worthy of it and then live accordingly. When we have done our healing work, self-love becomes second nature. And a lot of the things you struggle to do now, like saying no, setting healthy boundaries, and speaking up for yourself, will automatically become easier.

I share my story to support you on your own healing journey as well as be an example to you for how to live your own life. People will leave you; friends and family will get upset, and it's all okay. It is part of the healing journey. So continue to walk on your path, knowing that you are on the right track. Keep going on your journey, knowing you are going to find the most amazing treasure at the end … you.

Scan the QR code below for access to the
Healing Doesn't Look Like That worksheet to help
you with your own healing journey.

Thank you for reading *Healing Doesn't Look
Like That* by Taneshia Johnson, MSW
If you enjoyed this book or found it to be helpful, please
help spread the word by leaving an online review.

Keep in Touch with Taneshia Johnson, MSW
Website: www.tjselfcare.com
Facebook: https://www.facebook.com/taneshia.tj
Instagram: @TJSelfcare